Chhaunk

Chhaunk

On Food, Economics and Society

ABHIJIT BANERJEE

ILLUSTRATIONS BY
CHEYENNE OLIVIER

 juggernaut

JUGGERNAUT BOOKS
C-I-128, First Floor, Sangam Vihar,
Near Holi Chowk, New Delhi 110080, India

First published by Juggernaut Books 2024

10 9 8 7 6 5 4 3 2 1

P-ISBN: 9789353452421
E-ISBN: 9789353458089

Typeset in Calluna Sans by R. Ajith Kumar, Noida

Printed at Thomson Press India Ltd

Chhaunk

(Pronounced chh-on-k)

Also called 'tadka' (in Hindi, Punjabi, Urdu), 'vaghar' (Gujarati, Hindi) and 'phoron' (Bengali).

The process of tempering to finish a dish in Indian cooking. It involves spices being put in hot oil, which is then added to a dish to create an extra layer of flavour.

In Bengali, 'phoron kata' means passing a brief comment.

Contents

Author's Note

hy does an economist write about cooking? Why would he want to publish recipes? The quick answer is that I am greedy; I love eating. When I eat something particularly memorable or read about a dish that sounds especially intriguing, I often try to make it. My hands are not skilled enough for French pastries, and sometimes, I fail even with down-home desi dishes. I still recall with horror the sticky mess I made while trying to replicate the wonderful *methiche aalan* that the well-known Delhi obstetrician and extraordinary cook, Ruma Satwik, had made for us. But I do often figure it out (sometimes after multiple tries), and over the years, this process has taught me a lot about the pros and cons of different cooking techniques. In other words, I have learnt what makes for a good recipe.

But I don't know whether I would have found the time to write a cookbook had it not been for the enforced confinement of the pandemic. Cheyenne lived with our family through that strange period and, especially in the early days of swirling rumours about the impending Armageddon and the different shapes it would take, we found solace in planning complicated meals and executing them. Every day, around ten in the morning, I would show up in Cheyenne's room. She would look up from her drawing and ask, 'So, what are we cooking today?' We would discuss what was in the fridge, what might be available – this being the disrupted early days of the pandemic – and ultimately, though we tried not to articulate this thought to ourselves, how we could outdo the show we had put on in the past days.

The plan of working on a cookbook together emerged, inter alia, through those conversations. I had a collection of recipes that I had shared with friends and family, which could probably be turned into a cookbook, but it was nowhere close to being done. I showed the half-finished manuscript to Cheyenne, partly in the hope that she would take on the task of illustrating the cookbook. She was polite but blunt, very much like, now that I know her better, I would have expected her to be. In particular, she thought that the book did very little to connect to my identity as a development economist. Thankfully, she also signed up to work on it with me (after I promised to add more economics to the book).

When *Cooking to Save Your Life* came out, we were excited by the general public's reaction to it. Many of the interviews had thoughtful and interesting questions that forced me to try to articulate what is special about a cookbook written by an economist. In the process, it became clearer to me that I think of a meal like an economist thinks about most things: how does one get to a specific objective (impressing/indulging/comforting/nourishing a particular person or group of people) with minimum time and hard work? It obviously helps to have dishes that come with interesting stories; dishes that surprise the palate or trick the eye – ultimately, dishes that leave an impression well beyond the effort that went into their making. *Cooking to Save Your Life* had a lot of these. But it also had many everyday dishes; I could see that they were chosen because they evoked specific moments from my life.

After the book tour ended and the interviews died down, we realized that we would love to keep going. Writing and presenting the book had made us much more aware of all the ways in which talking about food was like talking about everything else in the world – from politics to history to economics to culture – in a way that does not need to be academic or polemical. It was a way to plant ideas in the soft soil of food memories and kitchen stories, where they can germinate and grow without necessarily provoking the kind of quick and sharp reaction that is characteristic of today's social media-driven world. It offered me an opportunity to reminisce, to go back in my mind to all the people and places, and above all, all the Indias that have been a part of my long life.

We thought of doing a blog, but quickly realized that even Cheyenne, despite her millennial status, was not really comfortable with the pace that it sets. We were lucky enough to get a chance to do a monthly column in the Sunday edition of *The Times of India*. We had an image of a reader on a slow morning, drinking sweet, milky tea and biting into a kachori redolent with hing or a still-warm idli enrobed in gunpowder, and that made us aim for a particular voice, slow and gentle but also rich and nuanced, enlivened by the vivid colours and shapes of Cheyenne's illustrations.

And that is how this book began about two years ago. Now that we have twenty-four columns, we can see that there are many recurrent themes that go back to our shared interests in the social sciences; themes at the intersection of economics, sociology, psychology and social policy that we have tried to draw out in the three new essays that we added to the collection of what were originally monthly columns. We have also added fifty-odd recipes that complement those that were at the end of each column and connect, in different ways, to that essay's themes.

We intend for this to be a very different book from our previous one – smaller, less ornate, more of a book to read rather than a cookbook. It is more about social science and ideas in general, with a wider range of recipes – from the unabashedly elaborate to the thirty-minute meals, from summer coolers to Christmas cakes. The organizing principle is that each essay offers an angle on the food (or drinks) that inspired the choice of the recipes that follow the essay. We hope the reading will inspire you to cook, and the cooking to read further.

PART I

ECONOMICS AND PSYCHOLOGY

Introduction

Since we published our previous book, two of the most important people in our lives are no longer with us. My mother, Nirmala, passed away in November 2023. Cheyenne's father, Bernard, left us in December 2023. They were, without doubt, the strongest influences on who we are. My mother was a professor; Bernard was a truck driver. But somehow, they were very similar people, at least in the ways they related to us: liberal, opinionated, loving, volatile, engaged with the world, and committed to living well. It is hard to think of their passing without thinking of how they live within us.

The ways our families and circumstances shape who we are, for better and for worse, fits well with one of the main themes in this book – why do we behave the way we do? Economics starts from the premise that the answer to these questions can be found in the pursuit of rational self-interest. Moreover, since self-interest, in principle, covers almost any kind of behaviour – if

I feel like donating the clothes on my back, as my great-great-grandfather once did (see 'Why Give Gifts?'), then that is my self-interest. Economists like to limit self-interest to one's pursuit of material well-being. One of the more exciting developments in economics in the last thirty years is the increased acceptance of the fact that most people are neither particularly self-interested (at least in that narrow sense) nor particularly rational, if rational means being able to effectively pursue that version of self-interest. This is the inspiration of the field that calls itself behavioural economics.

Several of the essays in this book are about why this can offer us a very different way of thinking about economic ideas. For one, while economists tend to think of preferences as being intrinsic and almost constitutive of who we are, behavioural economists emphasize the role of social pressures. Women's role in the world (whether they should work or stay at home, what they will do with an unwanted pregnancy, if they should wear a headscarf or not) is a subject on which society often feels comfortable to impose its heavy hand. My aunt was told that she should not take up the jobs she was qualified for because her in-laws would like her to stay home and serve them food.

The question is, to what extent are these the actual preferences of the husband or his family and to what extent is it just the socially appropriate thing to do? In a remarkable experiment published in the ultra-prestigious *American Economic Review*,[1] Leonardo Bursztyn, Alessandra L. González and David Yanagizawa-Drott show data that a vast majority of younger Saudi men are comfortable with their wives working but think they would face social censure if they actually went through with this decision. The authors informed a random sample of 250 young men that the views of others actually lined up with theirs and found that the wives of those so informed were much more likely to interview for jobs in the next few months.

When I told my mum this story, she was enthused but remained sceptical of her target group – Indian guardians of young women – behaving this reasonably. As I write in 'Women and Work', the chapter that marks her passing, my mother would keep coming back to how Indian families damage their daughters by obsessing about protecting their virginity until they can be 'handed over' to a husband's family 'intact', and that responsibility can then be shifted to the marital family. This overprotection is why, she argued, Indian women never get enough of a chance to enjoy their youth, find their vocation and become who they could be instead of the unpaid cook and cleaner of the household. I love cooking and I don't mind cleaning dishes, but I am sure many women, even in the US, play that role out of a sense of duty rather than a love for spending time in the kitchen.

Social pressures, of course, are not confined to gender relations. 'Mango and Manners' is about table manners and how they serve to reinforce social distinctions. We already know that about what people eat – upper-caste Hindus are much more likely to be vegetarian than other Indians – but it is equally true of how we eat. Being more aware of just how arbitrary our notions of good manners are, might help us become more tolerant.

Table manners, of course, are taught at the dinner table – my mother would calmly slap my elbows off the table because 'no elbows' was part of her education. In economic narratives, the dining table is a frequent metaphor for all the ways in which our parents mould us. Yet, as I write in 'Where Do Our Preferences Come From?', I learnt many things at the dinner table (not just where to put my elbows) – how to tell a story, how to take a joke against you (I am an easy target – now it is my kids who enjoy that), where the line between funny and nasty lies. But never how to choose a career or get better grades, or how to be patient with one's investments or frugal with one's budget. In other words, nothing that economists care about.

This does not mean that the family does not shape us. I am an economist; my parents were both economists. The dinner table conversations about why there was so much misery in the slums next door made me the kind of economist I am. But my parents did not intend for me to be an economist – they thought I should do something (even) more math-driven (like a mathematician, maybe). In other words, as I argue in 'Cultural Capital', it is cultural capital and not dinner-table instruction that makes us: the books that we had lying around the house, the conversations about them, and – why not – my mother's attempts to recreate minestrone and pasta al tonno with what she could find in the Calcutta (now Kolkata) of the 1970s. This is why I remain a firm believer in affirmative action. When people talk of how everything should be based on merit and not identity, I want to remind them of the enormous advantages of growing up in a middle-class, upper-caste family like mine.

Behavioural economics has another important side, where rather than bringing ideas from sociology into economics, there is an attempt to deepen economists' understanding of psychology. It is easy, for example, to say that human beings are rational maximizers, but it is often hard to know what that really means. Is it rational to plan to exercise every other day, knowing that it won't actually happen? The answer is not obvious: it *is* useful to have goals – even ones that you will never fully reach – because they can act as a reminder that you need to do more. On the other hand, failing all the time can be discouraging. Perhaps it makes sense to set the goals lower.

Once we recognize that there is no one 'rational' choice in many situations – no ideal exercise plan that we can automatically adhere to by an act of will – the question of how to make plans that real humans can more or less stick to assumes a central role. 'Commitments We Can Keep' deals directly with this, but 'Energy-Efficient Eating' makes a related point. Saving energy while cooking may sound like a pain, but it can also become an interesting game where you challenge yourself to make something delicious with minimal use of energy. Once you think about it, that idea has wings – why not get your children to compete with you to switch off the lights, to ensure that the air conditioning is not leaking out, that you are not making two trips by car when one would suffice?

Abandoning the garb of the fully rational woman/man also gives us the language to talk about stress, anxiety, depression and confusion. The piece titled 'Edible Distractions' talks about psychological strategies for dealing with COVID-19 – a lot of our succour came from cooking – but also their limitations. The piece titled 'The Burden of Age' was even more personal – about growing old and getting sick, feeling weak and losing control; about my grandfather and Cheyenne's father, as well as the increasing loneliness among the elderly in India and the plague of depression that seems to go with that. My mother lived more or less alone, but so do increasing numbers of the low-income elderly in rural India, and they, unlike my mum, do not have the advantage of someone whose job is to care for them.

Ultimately, for me, writing these columns is therapy. It allows me to revisit my childhood, my family, my many friends, my hopes and disappointments, and perhaps above all, the India that I love and never left. And through that, it allows me to discover just how much of the economics I actually trust – sometimes, I have to admit, without empirical warrant – links back to those very salient moments of my life. Read them, please, not only as something final and definitive but also as the tentative articulation of many thoughts and associations that I begin to discover in me.

Women and Work

I was in Kolkata for pujo this year and since my mother's cook was on leave, I picked a restaurant that seemed nice. My mother hated it. She was bothered by these very well-built young men – who seemed to be part of the staff but did very little – and was convinced that we had somehow stumbled on a drug den. Even their rich and mellow mutton korma, redolent with mace and kewra, did little to mollify her. I tried, in vain, to convince her that she had it backward: this place, I explained, will turn into a nightclub after dinner hours and these were the bouncers, there to protect the rest from the drunk and drugged up. She was too grumpy to concede, so I relaxed into the good (but very spicy) chhole.

That was the last time we went out for a proper meal. My mother, Nirmala Banerjee, passed away a week later. She was almost eighty-eight, but still, when she had the energy, like on that evening, immensely lively and feisty. I miss her all the time.

The next morning, she was in a more conciliatory mood, and conceded that nightclubs do need bouncers – when she was a student in England in the 1950s, they would often go out dancing and there would occasionally be trouble, and 'with Indian males these days . . .'. Given that rather dire assessment, it may be surprising that she was always and adamantly of the view that women need the chance to go out and enjoy themselves without the protective embrace of their fathers, brothers, husbands or lovers.

The paper she was working on when she passed away, tentatively titled 'Workers or Housewives?', returns to one of her recurrent themes: the role of the family in shaping the labour force participation of women in India. In most developing countries, young women tend to enter the workforce at the cusp of adulthood. They then quit to get married and have children, and perhaps return to outside work when their children are old enough. We see this in Bangladesh and China now, but it was also true of currently industrialized countries in their early days of industrialization.

India, she emphasized, is the one exception – women first get married and have children, before they consider seeking work. In other words, at the age where young women the world over are joining the workforce – learning the work routines and the discipline, gaining the confidence to speak up for themselves, but also embracing the pleasures, tight friendships, giggly lunchtime conversations – Indian woman are mostly at home, preparing to get married. It is then not so much of a surprise that most of them don't end up working

– India in 2022 had one of the lowest female labour force participation rates (LFPR) in the world, below, for example, Saudi Arabia.

'One important reason for this,' she wrote, 'seems to be the absolute social imperative for women to strictly contain their sexuality within marriage, preferably in a monogamous, socially approved marriage. Violation of this taboo by a woman, whether by choice or by some compulsion, is considered her ultimate degradation.' Parents worry that if their daughter goes out to work, especially if her work requires spending nights away from home, they might meet someone they like, or why not, just sleep with someone because they want to. Perhaps someone who is not fit to be a husband – already married, wrong caste, wrong religion, wrong gender, etc.

Or worse, they might end up being coerced into having sex. Or simply acquire a jilted lover or an angry aspirant, who goes around saying that they had sex, when she had been careful not to. The world believes what it wants to believe, and it does not help that she was seen coming back late a few times.

Her point was that in a world where women are judged by their 'purity' and 'sullied women' are deemed unmarriageable, families face a strong incentive to get their daughters married before they have a chance to go 'astray'.

My mother understood these compulsions very well; she was an academic but also an activist who helped create and run Sachetana, an NGO that fought for women's rights. A lot of its work was in our neighbourhood, a transitional area between a solidly middle-class area and a large slum. I have no reason to believe that the middle-classes behaved better, but they hid their secrets behind closed doors whereas the slum-dwellers had no such option. Domestic fights would spill over into the space in front of our house. He would start by calling her a slut, usually for complaining about his having spent the day's earnings on booze, and it would get more anatomically specific from there. More often than not, she would hold her peace to avoid provoking him further, but there were days when, to our delight, she would weigh in on his nightly performance (or lack thereof). My mother would be screaming at the top of her voice from our verandah – telling them to shut up and go home – in a vain attempt to protect us from the facts of life, while warning him that she would call the police if he hit her again.

Casting aspersions on a woman's virtue is what irate men do everywhere, but in South Asia, we take it a step further. Where else in the world would a man murder a daughter or a sister for the crime of liking someone better than the man the family had chosen for her?

As my mother never got tired of repeating, this protectiveness keeps women from finding a job without actually allowing them to take it easy. The economic pressure of a single-income family, often reinforced by reminders about who doesn't 'earn a living', creates a compulsion for women to contribute in every way they can. When they are not cleaning the house or cooking dinner for seven on a single burner, they wait on their in-laws or walk their children to school. In Rajasthan, they walk three miles in the sun to get water; in the lower delta of Bengal, they wade into rice fields, straining the standing water over and over through their pallu to catch a handful of little fish or shrimps. These might flavour a ghonto, the typically Bengali mélange of multiple vegetables cooked down in their own juices, for which they will also need to find some wild greens to pick.

While that sounds organic and vaguely romantic, my mother was adamant that this plethora of activities was a symptom of the problem. In her ideal world, each woman focuses on things that match her particular skills and, equally importantly, is recognized by the family as doing something important. It could be something inside the home, but for most of them, it will require stepping into the outside world.

And for that to happen, my mother insisted, we need to abandon our national obsession with controlling women's sex lives – teach them about contraception and the possibility of violence, she wrote in her last piece, but don't keep them locked in. There will be real risks, especially at the beginning, when you are the only woman out on the street at some late hour. But as more and more women take to the streets, it will become safer – as it was in the Mumbai that she grew up in. They will cook fewer wonderful ghontos but choose when to do so, and life will be sweeter for all of us.

These are the two dishes that I cooked during my last visit to my mum, a ghonto and a Bengali chana dal. I will brag a little – she said this was the best ghonto she had had in many months; the dal she said nothing about, but she took two helpings. She was a tough lady.

I added a dish I wanted to make (the mooli salad) that day, but she said it would be too much.

PALONG SAAGER GHONTO

200 GM TINY SHRIMPS (OR 15 SMALL VADIS FOR VEGETARIANS)

3½ TBSP MUSTARD OIL

3 CUPS SPINACH

1 CUP PUMPKIN

1 CUP EGGPLANT

½ CUP DAIKON (MOOLI)

1 GREEN CHILLI (SLIT)

2 TSP GRATED GINGER

1½ TSP TURMERIC

1 TSP FIVE-SPICE MIX (PANCHPHORON)

1¼ TSP SALT

½ TSP CAYENNE

▶ Start by marinating 200 gm of tiny shrimps with with ¼ tsp salt and ½ tsp turmeric for 15 minutes. (If you are a vegetarian, you can use 15 small vadis instead.) Fry them in 1½ tbsp of mustard oil for 2 minutes at medium heat. Turn off the heat and fish them out. Heat the remaining oil at medium high, add 1 tsp of the five-spice mix (panchphoron) and 1 slit green chilli. After 1 minute, add 1 cup each of the pumpkin and eggplant and ½ cup of daikon (mooli), all chopped into 1" cubes. Add 1 tsp each of salt and turmeric, and ½ tsp cayenne. Cover, set the heat to medium low and cook until the vegetables are melting (20–25 minutes). Add 3 packed cups of washed spinach leaves, and let them wilt and blend in. Add 2 tsp freshly grated ginger and the shrimps, cook for 2 minutes and remove from heat. If you are using vadis, break them into small pieces and use them to garnish the dish.

CHOLAR DAL

⅔ CUP CHANA DAL

⅔ CUP CHOPPED TOMATOES

¼ CUP RAISINS

4 TBSP FRESH COCONUT SLICES

2 TBSP GHEE

2 TSP GINGER PASTE

2 TSP GARLIC PASTE

4 CLOVES

4 GREEN CARDAMOM PODS

1" CINNAMON STICK

1 BAY LEAF

1 TSP TURMERIC

1 TSP CUMIN POWDER

1 TSP CORIANDER POWDER

1 TSP CAYENNE

1 TSP SALT

1 TSP SUGAR

 ▶ Pressure cook ⅔ cup chana dal till soft. In 2 tbsp ghee, cook 4 tbsp fresh coconut (cut into thin slices) till it starts to turn red. Remove from the ghee. In the same ghee, fry 1" piece of cinnamon, 4 cloves, 4 cardamom pods and 1 bay leaf for a minute and then add 2 tsp each of ground garlic and ginger. Fry for another minute, and add 1 tsp each of turmeric, cumin powder, coriander powder, cayenne and salt. After a minute, add ⅔ cup of finely chopped tomatoes and fry at medium heat for about 3 minutes till it's almost a paste. Add the chana dal (with its cooking liquid) along with 1½ cups of water and cook at medium low heat for 10 minutes. Add the fried coconut, ¼ cup raisins and 1 heaped tsp of sugar. Simmer for 5 minutes. The dal should now be sweet, savoury and a little spicy. Adjust the balance of sweetness and saltiness as per your taste.

NEPALESE DAIKON SALAD

2 CUPS GRATED DAIKON

¼ CUP CHOPPED TOMATO

¼ CUP THINLY SLICED RED ONION

1 GREEN CHILLI, FINELY SLICED

3 TBSP CHOPPED CILANTRO

FOR THE DRESSING

2 TBSP ROASTED AND GROUND SESAME SEEDS

2 TBSP MUSTARD OR SESAME OIL

1 TBSP GRATED TIBETAN YAK CHEESE (OR HARD FETA)

1 TBSP LEMON JUICE

SALT (TO TASTE)

 ▶ In a big salad bowl, add 2 cups of grated daikon, ¼ cup thinly sliced red onions, ¼ cup chopped tomatoes, 1 finely sliced green chilli and 3 tbsp of chopped cilantro.

For the dressing, in a bowl, add 2 tbsp of roasted and ground sesame seeds, 1 tbsp grated Tibetan yak cheese (or hard feta), 2 tbsp of mustard (or sesame) oil, 1 tbsp of lemon juice and salt (to taste). Mix well. Pour this dressing over the ingredients in the salad bowl and mix well; set aside for 10 minutes before serving.

The Burden
of Age

I met my grandfather when I was four and he was sixty-four. I remember thinking he was the oldest person I had ever met. I am now almost the same age as he was then.

My grandfather was bipolar: he would be joyous and energetic, and then, his mood would turn. When I first met him, he was on the downswing, his shoulders slumped and smile dropping off before it reached his eyes.

Now that my parents are gone, I probably won't find out what caused it. Was it some unforgiving brain chemistry, or something that happened in his life? His career as the headmaster of one of Kolkata's most prestigious schools – a government school as it happened – was over when I met him. Was it that? It scares me, now that a lot of my contemporaries are retiring (happily, it seems).

I have a full plan to resist retirement, but in the long run, it is not just the will to keep going. Our bodies take decisions for us. I can still vividly see the day when my father could no longer manage the (complicated) manoeuvre – getting the machhbhat from the thali to his mouth – that we do unthinkingly every day. My mother had to take over feeding him – he, who so loved being in control.

Or that day when I had dinner with the once-famous raconteur – then in the cruel clutches of Alzheimer's – who kept repeating the same story every five minutes, still perfectly narrated with all its dramatic pauses, but frightening exactly for that reason. His wife and family kept trying to cut him off but, for that evening, it was not working. Only the khujerer gurer payesh (rice kheer with date sugar), which he relished, offered some relief.

Cheyenne, who conceived of this column with me and illustrated it, had just lost her father. He was young, much too young to die. A truck driver, proud of his strength and manual skills, he reacted to his encroaching sickness with a combination of nonchalance, confusion and horror. Towards the end, his mouth was constantly dry – a side-effect of the medication – and he wanted liquids, preferring the wonderful Spanish soup gazpacho to heavier dishes. There would be tense conversations every few meals, with Cheyenne arguing that while gazpacho is lovely, it is light on calories and null on proteins. He was losing weight and needed to eat more nutritious foods. Eventually, they landed on boiled potatoes with lots of butter – Bernard grew up in Belgium, the home of the original 'French' fries and many other potato dishes.

The gradual loss of control over our bodies is, of course, as old as humanity itself (though it used to happen at a much earlier age). Perhaps, as a recompense, most societies accorded a special place of influence for 'elders'. They were the wise, the respected and the powerful; increased influence within the family (and sometimes within the entire community) seemingly compensated for their private frailty. The biggest beneficiaries were, unsurprisingly, older men of wealth or high social status. But in a lot of the households that I grew up with, the mother-in-law also wielded enormous power, at least as long as her husband was alive. I recall one particular lady who was a diabetic – her legs were affected so she could hardly get up – but from her position on the bed, she would order her daily menu of snacks and sweets. One day it would be papri chat followed by kanchagolla; the next day it could be puchhka – Kolkata's famously hot and tart answer to pani puri – served in her bedroom by a street vendor who came all the way up, followed by a densely sweet kesari chumchum. The whole family knew and worried about it, but nobody dared to really challenge her. The inevitable happened soon enough, unfortunately.

In the 1960s and 1970s, which is when my memories of the mother-in-law's power date from, most people I knew – mostly Bengali and middle-class – lived in joint families. Housing was scarce, decent jobs were few and far between, so it made sense for all the brothers and unmarried/widowed sisters to crowd into the old family house with their wives and children, sharing whatever little income there was. But living together meant conflicts and choices. Someone had to take decisions – this was often the source of power for the more senior members.

Towards the end of the 1970s, the joint family system started to splinter. More and more flats got built, making it easier for the better-off to move out of the family residence. The improving job situation further aided this shift, at least for the well-educated. Sometimes the parents moved in with one child and the family house was sold, sometimes they remained with the rump family. Either way, their role in managing the many fissiparous forces was diminished, and often, even the house they stayed in was no longer theirs. The senior couple was losing their central role in the family.

This was accentuated by demographic change. Families were having fewer and fewer children. This meant that the joint families were less joint, especially since it also became more common for middle-class children to move for employment. An increasing fraction of families had one or more children working in Bangalore, Bahrain or Boston. Many parents suddenly found themselves living mostly alone, as my mother did for so many years.

The same transition was also happening among the less well-off families, if at a somewhat slower pace. The number of children was dropping everywhere – the average fertility rate dropped from above four in the 1970s to about two in recent years nationwide. Rural–urban migration, though still low in comparison to other developing countries, was speeding up. As a result, the all-India proportion of elderly not living with children doubled between 2000 and 2010, and has surely gone up a lot since.

The world was also changing. The communication revolution and, in particular, the spread of cell phones changed attitudes and access to information. As kids, we relied heavily on my grandfather to tell us stories and, in the process, learnt a lot about his life and opinions. The Abhijit of today has access to audiobooks for stories; he is probably a little impatient with his grandparents' technological backwardness ('Dadu, you really know nothing.').

All of that means that today's elderly, who endured the heavy hand of their parents and big brothers when they were young, are now less important in the lives of their children and grandchildren. Despite our narrative about family-oriented India being entirely unlike the individualistic United States, the fraction of elderly who, in surveys, say that they are lonely, is similar in both countries – about 15 per cent. And in Tamil Nadu – which had an earlier and sharper fertility decline rate than North India, and is more urbanized – loneliness is much higher, closer to 30 per cent.

Those who say they are lonely are much more likely to be clinically depressed based on their responses to the standard set of diagnostic questions – depression rates among the elderly go from less than 20 per cent among those who say they are not lonely to more than 80 per cent among those who say that they are. Cause and effect are less clear – loneliness, especially if you were brought to expect a full family life in your old age, surely depresses people. But depressed people are difficult to care for, especially if their health is also failing, and even their nearest and dearest may find it difficult to spend time with them. Even Cheyenne, who devoted the last two years to taking care of her father, says that one of the hardest problems was that, half the time, he didn't know what he wanted. She would prepare something after a lengthy discussion with him, but when she served it, he realized he didn't want it anymore.

As the rest of India undergoes the same social transformation as Tamil Nadu, we will need policies to address the fast-rising tide of depression. While richer people are less depressed in general, a cash transfer to the elderly poor in Tamil Nadu had no durable effect on depression levels based on our randomized controlled trial, though maybe the amount of cash was too small. Nor was there any detectable benefit from therapy. Perhaps they need more ongoing engagements with people like them. It may be worth experimenting with regular events where they have tea with other lonely people of similar age. Maybe even a pot-luck meal, where they each contribute something? And while men may not know how to cook, anyone can learn, as I have written elsewhere. Why not these simple potato dishes for a start?

My daughter, Mimi, is a fan of both potatoes and strongly flavoured food. These are two of her favourites and, in a pinch, she can make them on her own, as long as I supply her with the boiled potatoes. Cheyenne often made mashed potatoes for her dad in his last year.

Potatoes offer an effortless comfort that people keen to, all over the world. They are also full of the kind of carbs that we are often warned against. Sweet potatoes are, perhaps paradoxically, less close to pure sugar than regular potatoes.

MIMI'S POTATOES WITH BLACK PEPPER

500 GM POTATOES
½ CUP FRESH CORIANDER LEAVES
6 TBSP SALTED BUTTER
2 TBSP CRUSHED BLACK PEPPER
1 TSP SALT

▶ Take 500 gm of boiled and peeled new potatoes (avoid using late-season potatoes, as they are distinctly sweetish). Smallish potatoes work the best for this preparation. In a large frying pan, heat 6 tbsp of salted butter at medium high. When the butter melts, add 2 tbsp of crushed (not powdered) black pepper.

After 40 seconds, add the potatoes along with 1 tsp salt and reduce the heat to medium. Mix well till the potatoes are nicely coated with pepper and fry for 5–6 minutes till they start to turn brown. Remove from heat, garnish with ½ cup chopped coriander leaves and serve.

LEEK-INFUSED MASHED POTATOES

500 GM BOILED POTATOES

TWO LEEKS

½ CUP SOUR CREAM

3 TBSP SALTED BUTTER

2 TBSP GHEE

1 TSP SALT

½ TSP BLACK PEPPER

 ▶ In a bowl, mash 500 gm of peeled and boiled potatoes (avoid using sweetish potatoes) with a potato masher or the back of a spoon while they're hot. Add 3 tbsp of salted butter, ½ cup sour cream, ½ tsp black pepper and 1 tsp salt into the bowl, and mix well.

Take two leeks, and cut the white and light green parts lengthwise into thin strips (about 1" long). Heat 2 tbsp of ghee and fry the leek strips until they turn brown at the edges. Pour this chhaunk over the mashed potatoes and mix well.

SWEET POTATO STEW

500 GM SWEET POTATO

3 CUPS CHOPPED KALE OR SPINACH

3 CUPS VEGETABLE STOCK/WATER

½ CUP THICK COCONUT MILK

⅔ CUP CHOPPED ONIONS

2 TBSP OLIVE OIL

2 TBSP MINCED GINGER

1 TBSP CHOPPED CILANTRO

2 TSP MINCED GARLIC

1 TSP CUMIN SEEDS

1 TSP CORIANDER POWDER

1 TSP ROASTED CUMIN POWDER

½ TSP TURMERIC

½ TSP PAPRIKA

1 SLICED LIME

SALT (TO TASTE)

▶ In a large pan, heat 2 tbsp of olive oil, and throw in 1 tsp cumin seeds and ⅔ cup of chopped onions. Soften the onions, and add 2 tbsp of minced ginger and 2 tsp minced garlic to it. After a minute, add 500 gm of sweet potato (peeled and cut into 1" cubes). Stir the pan to coat the potatoes in oil and throw in 1 heaped tsp of coriander powder, ½ tsp turmeric and ½ tsp paprika. Stir for 1 minute, and add 3 cups of vegetable stock (or water) and salt (to taste). Cover, lower the heat and let it cook for 30 minutes.

Add 3 cups of chopped kale or spinach and let it cook for 5 minutes, adding water or stock if required. Mash the potatoes slightly with the back of your spoon to thicken the gravy and then add ½ cup of thick coconut milk. Cook for 5 more minutes. Take the mixture off the heat. Garnish with chopped cilantro and roasted cumin powder. Serve with slices of lime.

Where Do Our Preferences Come From?

Where Do Our
Preferences Come
From?

Mealtimes are strange times. In our memories, they are often hallowed; a time of comfort and community. Your mother leaning over you, her face lit with love, dropping a dollop of homemade ghee on the steaming rice. Your father in his usual seat, face slightly closed but eyes sparkling like always when he has a great story to relate. The sweet steam from the hot *gobindobhog* rice surrounds you all.

That's how our brains often curate our memories. But when I try just a little bit harder, I can also remember the family dinner at my aunt's house where her mother-in-law didn't show up. Food was served for her but she was conspicuously missing from the seat from which she dominated the life of the family. A servant was sent up to investigate. She will not eat, she said. Not in a house where she was not respected.

I never found out who was to blame or what happened; I was too little to be part of the whispers around the table, but the fact that my aunt was the next to leave was probably not unrelated. We Indians fast for many reasons, but perhaps for that reason, the act of refusing food remains very potent. So much so that in Jawaharlal Nehru University (JNU), there was something called 'relay hunger strike'. We would sit around for a few hours at the protest site, not eating, and then would be relieved by someone else, free to fill up again. When I explained that idea to my radical American friends, I remember one of them almost falling off his chair in laughter.

But back to submerged memories. Some of you can probably recall the day when you had prepared the mutton korma with infinite care, the onions fried with cardamoms till deeply red but not yet crisp, turned into paste to be added to the sauce a few minutes before the dish was done, along with a few drops of kewra. Exactly how your daughter always loved it, but that day, with tears in her eyes and firmness in her voice, she said: 'Ma, I am not going to eat meat anymore.' Maybe you ate it alone, remembering that other day, some years ago, when the same daughter refused to eat any vegetables and insisted on eating plain rice with what looked like a shovelful of salt.

Mealtimes can be wartime.

Bengali movies and theatre rely heavily on the dramatic potential of mealtimes. The husband is back late, drunk and smelling of his evening with some lady of the night. The waiting wife immediately understands what has happened, quietly serves him his meal and then sits down with her thali but does not touch it. The question is: has he noticed? Formal dining scenes are, of course, also heavily used in the films of the great Spanish–Mexican filmmaker Luis Bunuel – who loved their ritualized quality – and as a climax in many happy and sad dramas, like that strange Danish film, *Babette's Feast*.

For economists, on the other hand, mealtimes are teaching times. Mealtimes are less about the drama and more a metaphor for the slow and repetitive process through which families shape the preferences of their children, including (but not limited to) the preference for food. There is obviously a lot of truth to this. I suspect there is nothing intrinsic about my love of bitter dishes: baingan with neem leaves, crispy fried karela rings dusted with aamchur, the wonderful Bengali vegetable stew *shukto*, flavoured with panchphoran and that perhaps uniquely Bengali spice called *radhuni* (a cousin of ajwain?) and a paste made from poppy seeds and mustard seeds. I suspect it was born of the routine of starting every meal with them, combined with occasional talk about how this was uniquely Bengali, plus some learned comments about the virtues of bitter foods in stimulating the liver. I also remember less successful attempts like trying to persuade my daughter that fruits are safe to eat even when they are not puréed and put into a plastic package.

This matters a lot to economists because economic methodology relies heavily on the act of choice. At a philosophical level, we often measure well-being by the things we purchase. At a more practical level, economists are often asked by courts to estimate the value of a statistical life (VSL), which is meant to be the just compensation for lives lost due to negligence, say by large private companies or the government.

One common way to do this is to compare the earnings of those who have less and more risky jobs – like garbage men and farmers on one side and miners and truck-drivers on the other – and calculate how much more say the miner gets paid for the extra life risk he bears. This, it is argued, 'reveals' the person's preferences over money and risk, to use the rather biblical vocabulary introduced by my late colleague, Paul Samuelson.

The underlying assumption here is that there is something innate and authentic that gets expressed in the choices we observe, somehow deeper than the sudden desire inspired by a billboard featuring a particularly luscious spoonful of ice cream. Hence, the emphasis on the theory that preferences are formed in childhood (or live inside our genes).

However, it is not clear to me if most things we learn at the dinner table (or, more generally, by being with our parents) are deep in the sense that economists would like it, essential to who we are as individuals. I, for example, grew up avoiding vanilla ice cream. This was because my dad really did not like vanilla – the result of his having worked in a Walls factory in his student days in London, where there was a pervasive and permanent miasma of synthetic vanilla. He told that story well and often, and somehow, that discouraged me. But on a trip to Italy, I decided to try affogato – a version of cold coffee with ice cream where the coffee is strong expresso and the ice cream is a wonderfully dense gelato – and totally loved it! I have since been a devotee to both the ice cream and the combo. I was also suspicious of chicken, largely because my mother never liked it much. But I now count roast chicken,

chicken butter masala and Hainanese chicken rice in the list of my favourite foods.

The point is that childhood preferences are often just that: childhood preferences, heavily influenced by parental opinions, positively or otherwise. My daughter rejects all vegetables not because she has evaluated all of them and decided that she could not possibly need or want any of their attributes, but because she heard that note of anxiety in my voice when they were proposed to her and inferred that vegetables were things kids are not supposed to like. The idea that we should all be respectful of what people want because it comes from those magic mealtimes seems a little fanciful to me (which is also why I continue to try to persuade my daughter). If there is a case for not interfering with people's choices, even when they make little sense to us ('why did she buy a TV with her savings and not a sewing machine?') – which I think there is – it should be based on how little we understand about the compulsions others face, rather than a judgment about how deeply thought-out the preferences are.

With the value of life calculations, there is an additional problem: mealtimes are meant to be relaxed times (even if they often are not); a brief respite from the tensions of the day. They are naturally times for what is exciting and heroic, funny and stupid. I suspect very few farmers or miners spend their dinner time on objective comparisons of risk and return associated with their two professions. While mealtimes may very well have a powerful influence on our lives, I suspect, paradoxically, it is precisely in the direction of propagating powerful myths and great stories, potentially away from economic rationality.

In our family, the sauce of Indian meat dishes ('jhol' in Bangla) has a particularly elevated status. The meat is mostly an inconvenience that we have to endure to be able to dip the phulka, roti or paratha in the sauce. Here are three very different ways to make jhol, each profiting from the very different flavour that the type of meat brings to it.

MUTTON KORMA

750 GM LAMB/MUTTON (GOAT)

400 GM ONIONS

250 GM YOGURT

4 TBSP OIL

4 BLACK CARDAMOM PODS

6 GREEN CARDAMOM PODS

12 CASHEW NUTS

2 TBSP GHEE

1½ TBSP GINGER–GARLIC PASTE

4 TSP TURMERIC POWDER

1 TSP SALT

½ TSP RED CHILLI POWDER

½ TSP KASHMIRI CHILLI POWDER

FEW STRANDS OF SAFFRON

 ▶ Heat 4 tbsp of oil in a large, heavy-bottomed pan and add 400 gm thinly sliced onions to it. Fry them till they start turning a deep red. Fish the fried onions out of the oil and set them out on paper towels to drain the excess oil.

In the same pan, fry 4 black cardamom pods and 6 green cardamom pods for a minute at medium low, and remove into a mortar and pestle.

Take a large pot and add 2 tbsp ghee to it. Raise the heat to medium high and add 750 gm lamb or mutton cut into small botis. Fry till the meat changes colour. Add 1½ tbsp ginger–garlic paste and fry for a minute. Then add 1 tsp salt, 4 tsp turmeric powder, ½ tsp red chilli powder as well as ½ tsp Kashmiri chilli powder and fry for another minute.

Add 250 gm yogurt that has been blended with 12 cashew nuts. Reduce the heat and cover the pot. Cook at medium low till the meat is tender. Crush the cardamom pods with your pestle, throwing out as much of the outer skins as you can. Add them with the fried onions to a food processor and pulse for a minute so that the onions are chopped but not a paste. Stir this mixture into the sauce, and let it simmer for 5 minutes. Remove the mixture from the heat, dribble some saffron water over it (if you have it) and cover.

CHICKEN DALHOUSIE

1 KG CHICKEN

1 CUP THINLY SLICED ONIONS

1 CUP CHOPPED TOMATO

1 CUP CORIANDER LEAVES

10 PEPPERCORNS

10 CLOVES

6 GREEN CARDAMOM PODS

2 BLACK CARDAMOM PODS

1" STICK OF CINNAMON

3 TBSP OF ANY PLAIN OIL (AVOID USING MUSTARD, OLIVE OIL OR PEANUT OIL)

1 TSP SALT

1 TSP TURMERIC POWDER

1TSP CUMIN POWDER

1 TSP CORIANDER POWDER

½ TSP CHILLI POWDER

 ▶ In a pan, heat 3 tbsp of oil and lightly sauté the chicken pieces at medium heat till white. Remove the chicken from oil, raise the heat and add whole spices (10 peppercorns, 10 cloves, 6 green cardamom pods, 2 black cardamom pods, 1" stick of cinnamon) to the same oil. Cook for 1 minute and then reduce the heat to medium. Add 1 cup thinly sliced onions and fry till they are golden.

Add 1 cup chopped tomatoes and the coriander leaves, 1 tsp each of turmeric powder, cumin powder, coriander powder and chilli powder along with salt (to taste). Cook at medium low till it turns into a sauce. Add 1½ cups of warm water along with the sautéed chicken, and cover and cook at medium low till the chicken is done. Thicken the sauce (if needed) by raising the heat and cooking for a bit longer.

BENGALI BEEF CURRY

1½ KG BEEF (CUT INTO 1" CUBES)

2 CUPS THINLY SLICED ONIONS

2 RIPE TOMATOES (CHOPPED)

4 TBSP MUSTARD OIL

1 TBSP GARLIC PASTE

1 TBSP GINGER PASTE

1½ TSP CORIANDER POWDER

1½ TSP CUMIN POWDER

1 TSP FENNEL POWDER

½ TSP CHILLI POWDER (OR MORE TO TASTE)

½ TSP FRESHLY GROUND BLACK PEPPER

6 GREEN CARDAMOM PODS

5 CLOVES

2 BAY LEAFS

1" PIECE OF CINNAMON

GINGER (JULIENNED)

SALT (TO TASTE)

▶ In a large pan, heat 4 tbsp of mustard oil. Add the whole spices and fry for a minute. Then, add 2 cups of thinly sliced onions and cook till they're brown. Toss in the beef along with 1 tbsp each of ginger and garlic paste, 1½ tsp of coriander powder, 1½ tsp cumin powder, 1 tsp fennel powder, ½ tsp chilli powder and ½ tsp freshly ground pepper powder, and fry till the mixture is brown.

Transfer everything to a pressure cooker and add the chopped tomatoes, salt (to taste) and 2 cups of water. Pressure cook at high heat for 15 minutes. Transfer the contents of the cooker back to the pan and let it simmer for 20 minutes. Adjust the salt and chilli as per taste, and garnish with thin strips of ginger.

Cultural
Capital

We ate dinner together in our family. The four of us and my grandfather. The staples of our conversation were 'one more boring meal' (usually me), 'India is winning/losing' (my brother), 'there is a new movie/song/play out' (me, my brother, my mother) and 'how could things get even worse for women?' (my mother). My father rarely led off on anything – his role was to find a humorous riff on whatever was being said.

Truth be told, we almost never got into an in-depth discussion – my dad's gentle, smiling cynicism set the tone of the conversation. Nonetheless, thinking back, I can see that this was often the first time I encountered many different ideas and tried to react to them, sometimes just to counter my dad's flippancy.

This is part of what sociologists call 'cultural capital'. We – my brother and I – not only learnt the right books to read and the right names to drop (and how), but also to connect ideas to names and names to other ideas. This is what conversations and narratives are built of. I am an academic, my brother an ad-man. We both market ideas, and what we learnt at the dinner table has served us well over the years.

The recent judgment of the US Supreme Court, undermining affirmative action in college admissions, made me think of that. Higher grades (and maybe better performance in extracurriculars) – and not the student's family background – should decide who goes to Harvard or MIT, though the phrasing of the judgment leaves some room for ambiguity. The underlying claim seems to be that we can ignore just how much good grades owe to the cultural capital emanating from a house full of books and generations of teachers behind him/her (like me) and to parents able and willing to ferry their child from chess to clarinet to coding lessons (like we do for our children). It asks us to forget just how much harder it is to excel with parents who work multiple menial jobs and never have time for long, chatty meals; who let the television be the morning nanny because they needed the rest; who never read books for fun because they never saw their own parents do so.

Students for Fair Admissions, the litigant in this landmark US case, want 'merit-based' admissions, something we also hear in India. I would probably resist this idea even if we could agree on a measure of merit since we have very limited ways of redistributing to disadvantaged groups and a great education is clearly one such time-honoured route. But it clearly also depends on what we mean by 'merit'. Even if we accept that merit is the potential for making the most of the educational opportunities in purely academic terms, why would we ignore what it takes to do well in difficult circumstances? Why shouldn't the ability to excel without generations of cultural capital and the upper hand from parents who can devote their lives to their children's advancement, not count as a sign of greater talent and future promise?

None of this says that affirmative action as currently practised in India or the US is perfect. Disadvantage comes in many forms: income clearly matters, partly because it buys the coaching classes and the tennis lessons. So does how the family earns that income: teachers may not be paid a lot, but they have the time and training to help their kids. Where you grew up matters, as the important work of Harvard Professor Raj Chetty and others[2] shows – it helps to have good public schools and other kids of similar intellectual inclinations. But the monstrous history of race- or caste-based discrimination casts its long shadow well beyond the differences in family income or location. For one, given the histories of exclusion in both these countries, only a very rare low-caste or black family has many generations of higher education behind it. There is also a lack of confidence, the result of a long history of being made to feel inferior, and often, a deficit in cultural capital.

It seems obvious to me that given all this, past exam performance (and other non-academic successes heavily influenced by parental effort) should not be the sole measure of merit. How much of the underlying injustice we can fix with affirmative action in admissions is, however, less clear, given that people still need to live lives outside the school's door. When I joined JNU for my master's in economics, the top group in the admission list included me – the child of two economics professors – but also a son of a farming family that had barely enough land to live on, and several others from SC/ST families that owned small businesses or held low-level government jobs in smaller towns, for whom Delhi was a remote and exciting place. They were very different from my Kolkata friends – equally bright, but much more political, with greater awareness of India's ground reality, the depredations of caste and poverty, and the way the system works and fails. On the other hand, they never talked about food – my daily obsession – faced with the disastrous hostel meals. Food was food. Most days there was enough rice and dal. You take what you get and move on. Perhaps grumbling about the cooking only makes sense to those who don't have to worry about paying the school fees or repairing the roof.

In my family, we talked a lot about food. My grandfather would wax eloquent about some fish he had had, usually not at our house. I would complain and my mother would get upset – we should be grateful for what we get, she rightly insisted. But she also tried, within the constraints of her limited budget and busy life, to make the food more interesting. We had a cook who produced perfectly competent dal–chawal; my mother contributed the occasional roast, pie or crumble, but also Marathi delicacies like suralichi vadi and pomfret bhujna. In return, I would be her faithful sous chef, peeling carrots and popping peas, but also watching carefully what she did and listening to her explanations. That is how I learnt to cook. Perhaps more importantly, it is how I started to acquire my alphabet of smells and tastes, of food words and words of appreciation, which changed my life. That vocabulary allows me, on and off through the day, to contemplate what I will cook or eat, and makes my everyday special. But it also opens the door to the world of food conversations, connecting me to people who might otherwise have no interest in me. Food talk is a social adhesive. In being brought up with it, I was privileged in ways that affirmative action will not directly fix: those who grew up – because they had no choice – treating food purely instrumentally, are robbed of something precious in life, and the social power that comes with it.

With my own children, I try to involve them in cooking. The idea is for them to learn how to cook, but also to participate in this cultural project of cooking and eating well that is so much the basis of my social existence. We are some distance from there: they are still very American, devotees of chicken nuggets and pasta, burgers and pizza, suspicious of the unfamiliar, especially if it involves vegetables. Being involved with the cooking, we hope, will change that. In my current plan, the first step was to up the voltage on the basic tomato-based pasta sauce; the second, add some sautéed kabuli chana to the mix. The final step, and I have yet to get there, is to combine the kabuli chana with some greens and the tomato sauce to make a really delicious sauce for adults. For the book, I have added another couple of child-friendly recipes.

CHICKPEA PASTA FROM PUGLIA

2 KG TOMATOES

500 GM COOKED CHICKPEAS (KABULI CHANA)

500 GM STEMMED SPINACH LEAVES/BROCCOLI RABE

1 CUP BASIL LEAVES

1¼ CUPS OLIVE OIL

2 GARLIC HEADS

1½ TBSP COARSE SALT

1¼ TSP CHILLI FLAKES

½ TSP FENNEL POWDER

A PINCH OF BLACK PEPPER

▶ Into a huge pot of boiling water, add 2 kg tomatoes and cook for 45 seconds. Fish out the tomatoes and plunge them into iced water. Touching them lightly with a knife will allow easy peeling. Once peeled, cut them into quarters and remove the core along with the seeds. Finely chop them and put them into a large heavy-bottomed pan with 1 tbsp coarse salt. Cook at low heat for 45 minutes, until the tomatoes' pieces are melting (if you are using high-quality, canned, crushed tomatoes, this step should only take 20 minutes). While the tomato cooks, heat 1 cup of olive oil with 1 tsp chilli flakes and one head of garlic, sliced in half through the middle (such that all the cloves get cut in half), at medium high heat. After 5 minutes, add 1 cup of loosely packed basil leaves and when they stop crackling, strain the oil and pour it into your sauce. Let it simmer for 5 minutes and take it off the fire. This is the not-so-basic tomato sauce.

Fry 250 gm of cooked chickpeas in 3 tbsp of olive oil (that has been infused with 1 tbsp of sliced garlic, ¼ tsp chilli flakes, ½ tsp salt and a pinch of black pepper) till they start to brown. Take the mixture off the fire.

Make a coarse paste using the leftover cooked chickpeas (250 gm), and cook it for 10 minutes in 1 tbsp olive oil, with ½ tsp fennel powder and the tomato sauce prepared earlier. This can be served as a pasta sauce with a topping of fried chickpeas (prepared in the earlier step).

While the chickpeas are being fried, add 500 gm of stemmed spinach leaves or the same amount of pre-blanched and chopped broccoli rabe (not broccoli), and use this as a mix-in with the pasta sauce.

SWEET POTATO GNOCCHI

2½ CUPS FLOUR + EXTRA FOR FLOURING THE SURFACE

1 EGG

1 SWEET POTATO (500 GMS)

½ CUP RICOTTA

½ CUP UNSALTED BUTTER

4 TBSP HAZELNUTS OR PISTACHIOS (BROKEN)

2 TBSP OLIVE OIL

2 TBSP MINCED SAGE

1 TBSP MINCED GARLIC

1 TSP SALT

PARMESAN (TO GRATE OVER THE GNOCCHI)

PEPPER (TO TASTE)

 ▶ Take a sweet potato and pierce it all over with a fork. Wrap it in aluminium foil and bake in an oven for 1 hour at 200°C till soft. Peel, mash and mix it with ½ cup ricotta, 1 egg, salt and pepper. Into this mixture, slowly incorporate 2½ cups of flour and knead lightly.

Flour the surface you will be using and on it, make sausages out of the dough (about 1" in diameter) and cut them into ½" pieces. Put these pieces into boiling salt water for 5 minutes till soft and then fish out with a slotted spoon. This is the gnocchi.

Heat 2 tbsp of olive oil in a pan and fry the gnocchis till they turn golden brown and crispy, then fish out with the slotted spoon. In the same pan, slowly melt ½ cup unsalted butter and add 1 tbsp minced garlic. After 45 seconds, add the hazelnut pieces and 2 tbsp of minced sage. Add the gnocchis back into the pan and coat with the flavoured butter. Serve with grated parmesan and several turns of a pepper grinder.

APRICOT COMPOTE

1 CUP DRIED APRICOTS

2 TBSP HONEY

1 TBSP SPLENDA OR SUGAR

1 VANILLA POD OR 1 TSP VANILLA ESSENCE

▶ Soak a cup of dried apricots in 2 cups of warm water for about 20 minutes. Strain out the water and set aside. Chop up the apricot into matchstick-sized slices.

Into a pan, add the strained water from earlier, along with the apricot slices, 2 tbsp honey, 1 tbsp Splenda/sugar and 1 vanilla pod (or 1 tsp vanilla essence), and bring to a boil. Reduce the heat to low and simmer for 40 minutes till the mixture dries into a spoonable but thick sauce. Serve with curd.

Mangoes and
Manners

It's been so long ago that I no longer remember where I was going and why. It was a local train, one of those green and yellow compartments with an open door divided by a single metal bar. It was summer. A sanyasi, naked from the waist up, boarded the train and placed himself on the ground, right in front of the door. As the train left the station, he fished a yellow-orange mango out of his crotch and proceeded to knead it between his strong brown hands. After a while, satisfied that it was mushy enough, he bit the top of the mango and proceeded to suck out the flesh. Juice dribbled out onto his beard, but he made no attempt to wipe it off. I had never seen anyone eat a mango like that. I now know that there is a kind of mango, called *chushi* (which means 'to suck' in Bangla), meant for that treatment, but the intimacy with which he held it in his hands and especially the way he pursed his lips, left little to the imagination. At no time did he look at any of us, but one could not but feel that he was putting up a performance.

What did he want us to notice? That there was delight in his life, notwithstanding his bare chest and matted hair? That pleasure has no necessary connection with elegance (indeed, his whole act had its own elegance, just not the bone-China kind). He didn't explain.

Table manners were probably invented precisely to prevent such unabashed displays of carnality. What is considered appropriate behaviour at mealtimes in the West has changed drastically since the Middle Ages. Medieval banquets seem to have been hearty affairs with much carousing, dancing and music, and many meat dishes. I counted at least a dozen different meat courses in a banquet thrown by King Richard II of England for the Duke of Lancaster, including pig's heads, roasts of swans, wild boar, partridges, larks, cranes, rabbits, oxen, herons and a jelly of deer brawn (meat, I assume). Meat was hacked off the bone with knives that the guests brought with themselves and eaten by hand. Drinking cups were shared, the table or a slice of bread was used as the plate, and spoons were counted before the guests were allowed to leave. Enormous amounts got eaten, vats of alcohol got consumed and perhaps unsurprisingly, given all that, there was a fair amount of 'wenching' (including the notorious feast of the chestnuts, organized at the behest of Pope Cesare Borgia, where a hundred naked prostitutes were present).

Of course, the more extreme possibilities are the ones that get recorded – most actual dinners were surely tamer affairs. Medieval historians also emphasize that there were many attempts, by clerics and others, to instil a code of decorum in the diners, though this might just tell us that there was a problem. The twelfth-century text, *Book of the Civilised Man* (*Urbanus Magnus* in Latin) by Daniel of Beccles, somehow reached my mother, who, like Daniel, used to insist: 'do not put your elbows on the table.' Daniel goes on to say, 'you may do so at your own table, but not if you are visiting another.' My mother was less tolerant.

Nonetheless, medieval banquets were probably a far cry from the prissy peaks of Victorian dinner parties where the legs of the tables were sometimes wrapped in cloth to conceal the 'suggestive' sight of bare legs, and there was a different fork or spoon for every course. Some of this change was probably driven by economics and hygiene – when people could afford more tumblers, there was no need to share. As cutlery became more affordable, perhaps the advantage of avoiding grease on one's hands (since hot water to wash it off was still scarce) encouraged the move to forks and knives for eating. Or to reverse that logic, maybe the reason why we, in India, eat with our hands has something to do with the fact that the water is rarely too cold to wash off the grease. For me, eating with my hands is so natural that I keep hoping that the ready availability of hot tap water would start a trend in the West, but for now, our children seem to be the only converts. As you might imagine, this creates some tension (mostly for me) when we get invited to other, more conventional homes and our children proceed to pick up the meat with their fingers.

What is clear, however, is that these norms cannot all be explained by what is efficient to do. In the West, there is an uncomfortable awareness of the fact that even grown-up Indians eat with their hands, but the idea that there are multiple ways to do so is mostly foreign. We, in our family, were taught that the food must not touch any part of the hand beyond the upper digits, but my brother's ayah, I noticed, ate with her whole palm. Some years later, I saw Gautam Ghosh's powerful film *Dakhal*, where, in the celebratory eating scene that is the fulcrum of the film, the migrants are shown squeezing the rice with their whole hands and licking them down, in a way that would have earned a scolding in our middle-class brahmin milieu. In both cases, however, hands need to be washed before and after eating. It is not efficiency that dictates the difference – the way we eat must tell the world who we are, and equally importantly, who we are not. Table manners are all about caste and class.

Likewise, the shift away from eating with one's hands in Europe was part of a general cultural move towards self-restraint – in bodily functions (no more farting and belching in public), in the expressions of sexual appetite, in violence against animals and other human beings; the animal now came to the table pre-carved rather than getting hacked into pieces then and there. My instinct is to connect it to the fact that, until fairly recently, to be regal was to be virile. Kings were meant to be strong (in terms of their bodies and their will), sexually potent and great gorgers. The display of appetite and strength was a part of the legitimation process. The rise of more managerial models of what it means to be a leader (or a king, perhaps) contributed to the move towards displaying more restraint and competence. Perhaps Putin and Trump will move us back to the old ways.

To be clear, I am in no way implying that there is a universal pattern where societies become increasingly mannerly over time. In fact, when I am in Lucknow, talking to people my age or older, the loss of the old *tehzeeb* – the elaborate courtesies that permeated Hindu and Muslim urban culture in the nineteenth and early twentieth century – comes up a lot. The point is, as the great French sociologist Pierre Bourdieu would say, manners are a habitus – something very specific to a particular subculture that the participants assume to be natural and organic, but in fact, are a product of their upbringing (my mother slapping my elbow off the dinner table) and the broader economic circumstances that fed into it (we had a table and my parents had lived in the UK for some years). We look down on those who behave differently, especially if they happen to be socially unfavoured, and imitate those in positions of influence. In the great Bengali comic writer Parashuram's *Ulot Puran*, India has conquered Britain, and Britain's Indian-appointed governor wants to eat mangoes like the Indians do, and is hiding in the toilet, dripping with mango juice, practicing. I can eat mangoes with a fork like the French do, cutting them into neat cubes on a plate, but lasciviously licking my lips like that sanyasi, much as I would like to, still feels very alien. We surely have enough distinctions in the world without the entirely unnecessary ones created by our notions of good table manners?

The main recipe for this month is a savoury custard made with eggplants and eaten cold. It is a traditional Provençale recipe that I modified to suit my Indian palate. The mango chutney does a lot to perk this delicate dish up, and equally importantly, it makes it look like a French-style pastry. You can eat it with a knife and fork on a bone-China plate or with your fingers like a dhokla.

I added a couple more savoury mango-based recipes, combining mangoes with a milk product in very different ways.

MANGO-GLAZED PAPETON

5 EGGPLANTS (1500 GM)

4 EGGS

2 SWEET MANGOES (ABOUT 250 GM EACH)

⅓ CUP MILK

4 TBSP OLIVE OIL

2 TSP FINELY CHOPPED GARLIC

1 TSP TAMARIND PASTE

1 TSP KALONJI

½ TSP BHAJA MOSHLA

⅓ TSP METHI SEEDS

1 SLIT GREEN CHILLI

A SPRIG OF CURRY LEAVES

FRESHLY GROUND BLACK PEPPER (TO TASTE)

A PINCH OF TIKHA MIRCHI POWDER SALT (TO TASTE)

FOR BHAJA MOSHLA

2 TSP CUMIN SEEDS

2 TSP FENNEL SEEDS

¼ TSP METHI SEEDS

 ▶ For the papeton, cut 5 eggplants (1500 gm) lengthwise in half. Using a sharp knife, cut the flesh into a cross-hatched pattern without piercing the skin. Drizzle 1 tsp of olive oil on each half and sprinkle salt on them. Bake the eggplant halves, cut face up, at 200°C for 30 minutes or till fully done. Scoop out the flesh, discarding the dark seeds. Leave it a bowl for 10 minutes to cool and lose water. Pick up the flesh with a slotted spoon (leaving the water behind) and run it through a blender until it is smooth but not yet a paste. Heat 2 tbsp of oil and add 1 tsp kalonji, 1 slit green chilli and curry leaves into it. After 40 seconds, reduce the heat and add 2 tsp finely chopped garlic. After a minute, add the eggplant flesh and cook for 2 minutes, continuing the stirring. Remove from the heat and let it cool. Into this eggplant mixture, beat in 4 eggs along with ⅓ cup milk. Put the entire mixture in a heavy 8" baking dish (buttered) with the bottom lined with a cooking sheet. Taste it for salt and mix in some freshly ground black pepper. Put the baking dish in a larger pan with ¼" standing water and bake for 30 minutes at 180°C till it sets. Let it cool and then place it in the fridge to chill overnight.

To make bhaja moshla, in a pan, dry roast 2 tsp cumin seeds, 2 tsp fennel seeds and ¼ tsp methi seeds for 3 minutes at medium low heat. Remove from the heat, allow it to cool and grind into a powder.

For the mango chutney, take 2 sweet mangoes (about 250 gm each) and cut their two sides off. Make a crosshatch pattern on each side and open it up so that you can scoop out the flesh in little cubes. Sprinkle salt on these cubes, heat your broiler and broil them for 2–3 minutes until they start turning black in spots (or do the same thing using a dry-heated pan). Heat 1 tsp oil in a small pan, add ⅛ tsp of methi seeds and then, add the mango cubes with 1 tsp tamarind paste dissolved in 1 tbsp water, and a pinch of spicy red chilli powder. Mix well, taste for salt and sweet and mix in ½ tsp of bhaja moshla.

When the custard has fully cooled, transfer it on to a nice serving plate, discard the cooking sheet and paint the top with the mango chutney. Serve in wedges.

BURRATA WITH TWO MANGO SAUCES

1 FRESH BURRATA (250 GM OR MORE)
½ CUP MANGO CHUTNEY (REFER TO THE PREVIOUS RECIPE)
2 TBSP NON-SWEET MANGO PICKLE
1 TBSP OLIVE OIL

 ▶ Chop the mango pickle finely and mix with 1 tbsp oil (add a little extra oil, if needed, to make the mixture runny). Place the burrata on a plate, spoon the mango chutney over the burrata and then dribble the pickle sauce over it to make green-yellow streaks.

MANGO PACHADI

1 CUP CHOPPED MANGO

1 CUP YOGURT

⅓ CUP GRATED COCONUT

1 SHALLOT

1 SLIT GREEN CHILLI

2 TBSP CANOLA OIL

1 TSP MUSTARD SEEDS

1 TSP URAD DAL

1 DRY RED CHILLI

A SPRIG OF CURRY LEAVES

A PINCH OF HING (ASAFOETIDA)

SALT (TO TASTE)

▶ Take 1 cup of mangoes chopped into ½" cubes. In a wok, heat 2 tbsp of canola oil and add 1 tsp mustard seeds, a pinch of hing, curry leaves, 1 tsp urad dal and 1 dry red chilli into it. Next, add 1 chopped shallot and cook till its soft. Add the chopped mangoes and 1 slit green chilli to the mixture, and cover and cook on low heat till the mangoes are completely soft. Add ⅓ cup of grated coconut and cook for 2 minutes. Take the mixture off the heat and add 1 cup yogurt and salt (to taste).

Edible
Distractions

The pandemic started exactly four years ago (from when this was written). The first known case is from 8 December 2019, which means the virus was circulating Wuhan that November.

I think I first noticed that the pandemic was getting to me when Cheyenne, who lived with our family through the pandemic, caught me washing carrots and turnips (that had just been delivered) with Lysol, which is a powerful and poisonous disinfectant. It was probably not accidental that Donald Trump had proposed injecting Lysol (or something similar) into COVID-19 patients, to the horror of the medical community and the amusement of our whole family. But there I was . . .

We were, of course, among the most fortunate. We continued to be paid our generous salaries for some Zoom lectures delivered from the safety of our home office, unlike the doctors and nurses, municipal workers, delivery agents and so many others who had to risk their lives to do their jobs. Or the urban daily wage workers in India, who were suddenly jobless and forced to walk hundreds of kilometres back to their villages. Our house was large enough to allow seclusion when we wanted it. Most importantly, we all got along – the (many) hours spent in each other's company were pleasurable rather than being a burden.

There was still plenty of bad news, of course. The very first days of COVID-19 in Belgium claimed Cheyenne's grandmother. During India's horrific second wave, I would spend what felt like hours agonizing about what to write to the many who had lost their loved ones. It was even more difficult to ask that indelicate, typically American question, 'how is it going?', when the answer might easily be: 'it's stopped; it's over'.

On the other hand, after years of complaining that I needed more research hours, I finally had endless days to kill. The problem was that my mind was refusing to cooperate – it was easier to scour the news sites, vainly looking for signs of a return to normality, than to sit down and work.

Different people find different ways to kill time. Everyone around my mum was worrying about how to shop safely, so she got busy organizing a way to get fresh vegetables delivered. With the help of a friendly NGO, she got vegetable growers from villages just south of Kolkata to bring a truckload of their produce, every few days, for sale in the parking lot of her building.

Somewhat ironically for me in the US, when I decided to cook more to stay sane, ingredients were exactly the problem. Shops were closed. We had made a mad dash to the Indian store a day before it all closed down, which was when we first started asking ourselves the 'how long' question – just how many bags of mustard seeds or frozen coconut would be enough to ride out the apocalypse? We got used to ordering online, but that was more of a Soviet-style lottery ('Seven of the nine items you ordered are not available at this time') than red-blooded American consumerism ('Don't you want these, too?').

But compulsion is a great teacher. The young Hindu widows in nineteenth-century Bengal, denied the right to pleasure in any form, sentenced to a life without meat or fish (and sometimes, even onion and garlic), evolved an entire defiantly sensual 'widow's cuisine'. Our constraints were much milder, of course, and we didn't have quite that level of creativity either. Fortunately, there was the internet, which we scoured for recipes using whatever we had at hand (carrots, cabbage and canned beans, for example) and found many: some wonderful, some ill-conceived or poorly described and some very strange, indeed. We learnt fast whom to trust and what to avoid, and how to tweak recipes to make them align with our taste. Eventually, we even began to record our own 'inventions' in a notebook. Rereading it, it is easy to see our desperate need to keep the quest interesting – there was a week, for example, when we decided that the ingredients should be alliterative, as in a salad of cherries, chard and cheddar.

Silliness was part of what helped us stay sane. The World Health Organization (WHO) says that mental health problems worldwide might have gone up by as much as 25 per cent during the pandemic, though they recognize that there is a great deal of uncertainty around that number. It is easy to see why: for one, collecting reliable measures of mental health is hard when all data collection had to be over the phone or online. Respondents who didn't want to answer probing personal questions, perhaps because they were very depressed, could always hang up. Moreover, it was not enough to find that people were sad or anxious – we needed a way to compare that with how they would have been in the absence of the pandemic.

Alice Kassens and William Rodgers, both associated with the Federal Reserve Bank of St. Louis, used the US census bureau's relatively high-quality data on mental health during the pandemic to compare how different states fared over time. They found, not surprisingly, that anxiety levels went up when the number of cases or deaths in a state went up as compared to other states in the US, but also when the state unemployment rate surged or the lockdown was more severe. All of this makes sense: friends were dying, firms were closing, couples, forced to live in each other's hair, were fighting. Old people suffered the loneliness of forced isolation, children missed their schools and schoolmates.

What I would not have predicted was that the highest anxiety levels were among young adults (between the ages of eighteen and twenty-four) and especially among young women. This echoes the findings in the WHO report[3] and studies from various other countries. Even more surprisingly, for this group, neither the severity of COVID-19 nor the lack of jobs and opportunities to go out made any difference. They were just sad.

Some part of this could be that they are just more in touch with their feelings and more willing to acknowledge their anxieties – this accords with the findings of other, more qualitative studies. And once you think about it, this makes a certain amount of sense. Young adults faced limited serious health risks from COVID-19. Many of them were still studying and (during the pandemic) living with their families, so unemployment was also not so much of an issue. On the other hand, their sense of a normal progression in life, from school to a job to falling in love and settling down, was violently interrupted. And the future of the world – the world they expected to inherit and make their own – suddenly turned less secure. It was life, it seems, and not death that they were worrying about.

Moreover, perhaps more than any other group, they felt the weight of free time. We had children to keep us amused (or perhaps the other way around), a house to maintain, and breakfasts, lunches and dinners to prepare. Someone I know finally cleaned his basement freezer. Another painted her house. The young, on the other hand, perhaps did very little since they were probably being fed (by mum or Uber Eats) and if the cliché is to be believed, didn't spend a lot of time cleaning. Instead, they moped.

But as we move into a world of multiple new anxieties, with climate change and the AI revolution directly hitting the way we live, and COVID-19 still lurking, it is the young I worry about the most. They have the advantage of being less distracted by the immediacy of life and therefore, are better able to see themselves as a part of a greater humanity. For exactly this reason, when the world seems more fragile, it is they who will bear the most stress.

I imagine one of these young women or men at the end of another week filled with upheavals and crises, thinking about what they could make to occupy themselves for a chunk of time, without adding more stress to their lives. One recipe we discovered during the pandemic that fits this bill is for Carrot Kibbeh, a vegetarian version of the wonderful Middle Eastern ground meat and bulghur wheat (dalia) dish. A layer of carrot purée, infused with spices and mixed with bulghur and drained yogurt, is baked on a bed of Swiss chard or beet greens cooked with raisins and pine nuts. It is easy, but there are many small steps that take time, and the result is both delicious and showy enough for a nice dinner with friends.

Cooking complicated dishes was very much part of our COVID-19 strategy. Here are three examples. The macaroni dish is simpler but my daughter wanted to participate in its making, which made it doubly rewarding.

CARROT KIBBEH

2 CUPS YOGURT

1½ CUPS DALIA

750 GM CARROTS

500 GM BEET GREENS/SPINACH

½ CUP ONION

1 RED PEPPER

1 CLOVE GARLIC

3 TBSP GHEE

2 TBSP OIL

2 TBSP RAISINS

3 TBSP BROKEN CASHEW NUTS/PINENUTS

2 TSP TOMATO PURÉE

2 TSP SALT

1 TSP KASHMIRI CHILLI POWDER

▶ Put 2 cups of yogurt in a cheesecloth and let the liquid drain out. This should take about 2 hours. When that is mostly done, boil 750 gm of carrots (for about 20–25 minutes) till they're soft enough to purée. While the carrots are boiling, take a pan and roast 1½ cups of dalia in 1 tbsp ghee (for about 2 minutes) till it's aromatic and starts changing colour. Take out the dalia and set aside. Next, purée the boiled carrots a blender with a clove of garlic, 1 tsp salt and 1 tbsp ghee.

In the same pan, sauté ½ cup finely chopped onions and 1 red pepper chopped into peanut-sized pieces in 1 tbsp ghee at medium low heat till the onion turns translucent. Add 2 tsp tomato purée and 1 tsp Kashmiri chilli powder to the onion mixture and cook till nicely blended (for about 1 minute). Then add the carrot purée, ½ tsp salt and 1½ cups water. Add the dalia and cover tightly, bringing it to a boil and immediately reducing the heat to a simmer. Slowly add water in measures of ½ cups (depending on how big the grains are) till the dalia is cooked. The mixture should have the consistency of a dry khichdi, so don't add too much water. While it is cooking, fry 500 gm of finely chopped beet greens (or palak) in 2 tbsp oil (with ½ tsp salt) till they are wilted. Add 2 tbsp raisins and 3 tbsp broken cashews (or pinenuts) and fry till the mixture is fully dry and shrunken. To finish the recipe, preheat the oven to 200°C. In a 9" baking pan, put half the carrot purée, a layer of cooked greens, a layer of drained yogurt, and then add the rest of the carrot purée. Bake for 30 minutes.

EGG BIRYANI (SOUTH-INDIAN STYLE)

2 CUPS CHOPPED ONIONS

1½ CUPS SLICED ONIONS

1½ CUPS RICE

1 CUP COCONUT MILK (NOT TOO THICK)

6 EGGS

4 TBSP OIL

1 TSP MUSTARD SEEDS

3 GREEN CHILLIES (SLIT INTO HALVES)

1½ TSP FINELY CHOPPED GINGER

1½ TSP FINELY CHOPPED GARLIC

½ CUP CHOPPED TOMATOES

½ CUP GRATED COCONUT

1 TBSP LEMON JUICE

1 TBSP GHEE

1 TSP CUMIN SEEDS

1 TSP TURMERIC

1 CINNAMON STICK

3 CLOVES

3 GREEN CARDAMOM PODS

½ TSP CRUSHED PEPPERCORNS

½ TSP SAFFRON THREADS

¼ CUP WARM MILK

A SPRIG OF CURRY LEAVES

A PINCH OF HING

FOR GARNISH

FRIED ONIONS (FROM ABOVE)

FRIED CASHEW NUTS (OPTIONAL)

▶ Fry 1½ cups of sliced onions till they turn brown and set them aside. Boil 6 eggs for 10 minutes, peel them, make slits on all sides and sprinkle salt on them. Prepare the coconut milk (unless you are using canned coconut milk). Wash the rice and soak in cold water.

Heat 4 tbsp of oil in a pan and add mustard seeds. When they stop popping, add a pinch of hing, 2 cups of chopped onions, a sprig of curry leaves and 3 slit green chillies. Cook till the onions soften and add 1½ tsp of finely chopped ginger and 1½ tsp of finely chopped garlic. Sauté the mixture. Next, add ½ cup of chopped tomatoes and cook until they soften.

Blend ½ cup of grated coconut with 1 tsp cumin seeds and ¼ cup water. Add 1 tsp turmeric. Add this mixture to the pan and cook for 5 minutes till the liquid almost dries up. Add 1 cup of coconut milk (not too thick) and 6 boiled eggs to the pan, and cook for about 5 minutes at medium heat. Cook till the gravy thickens to a creamy texture (ensuring it is not too runny).

To prepare the rice, soak 1½ cups of rice in water and drain after 15 minutes. In a big pan, boil 4 cups of water with 1 stick of cinnamon, 3 cloves, 3 pods of cardamom, ½ tsp crushed peppercorns, 1 tbsp lemon juice and 1 tbsp ghee. Once the water starts boiling, add the soaked rice and cook for exactly 7 minutes. Drain the rice. In the meantime, soak ½ tsp saffron threads in ¼ cup of warm milk for 10 minutes.

To layer, place a bed of rice over the egg curry in the pan and make holes in it. Drizzle the saffron milk over the holes and arrange some of the saffron threads over the rice. Garnish with fried onions and fried cashew nuts. Cover the pan tightly and put it into the oven for 30 minutes at 125°C or on a tawa on low heat.

MACARONI AND CHEESE

500 GM MACARONI

250 GM GRATED TOMME/CHEDDAR

250 GM GRATED COMTE/EMMENTHALER/GRUYÈRE

200 GM GRATED PARMESAN

3 CUPS MILK

1½ CUPS BREADCRUMBS

2 TBSP BUTTER

2 TBSP FLOUR

▶ Cook the macaroni and set aside. Preheat the oven to 175°C. Mix together the grated tomme (or cheddar), comte (or emmenthaler/gruyère) and half the parmesan cheese. Mix the breadcrumbs with the rest of the grated parmesan.

In a pan, melt 2 tbsp of butter at low heat and whisk in the flour, making sure it does not burn and there are no lumps left. Add milk to the flour mixture, stirring continuously, and heat till it begins to send up vapours. Then add the cheese mix and let it melt into the milk, before adding in the boiled macaroni. Remove from the heat, pour it into a baking dish and cover with the cheesy breadcrumbs. Bake for 30 minutes.

Commitments
We Can Keep

I am at an age where there are only two people who really scold me – my mother and my doctor. 'You have no butt left,' my doctor told me, referring to the fact that I, like many Indian men of a certain age, have become increasingly one-dimensional. 'And you need that cushioning when you slip on the ice.'

She suggested six small protein-rich meals a day. I tried. I made it my new year's resolution for 2021 and invested in varieties of dietary supplements popular on the internet, only to discover that protein shakes have a viscous quality that gave me the feeling of drowning in a pool of petrol, and the low-sugar protein bars seemed to have an uncanny resemblance to (artificially) sweetened sand. I gave up on 4 January.

This is, of course, something that anyone who has tried to break a habit ('no more ice cream', 'exercise every day', 'I will never call her again' and of course, the classic, 'that's my last cigarette') knows well. It's easy to commit; it's hard to stick to that commitment.

Economists call this the 'dual-self' problem. There's your present self, who takes great pride and pleasure in announcing to the world (and, indeed, to themselves) their plan to lose five kilograms. Starting tomorrow. And then there is your future self, who agrees as long as it starts a day later. You can see where that can end up.

But even if you get started, the other self is still there, lobbing temptations in your way – 'you can't get cancer from just one more puff, can you?', 'Why not call her just one more time; it's been a week, maybe she is starting to miss you?', 'It's just one parantha, just ten grams of ghee – and so delicious – how could that matter either way, given that your goal is five kilograms?'

You are resolute – you fight back and turn away from the temptation. But it can be a pyrrhic victory; it is exhausting to deny oneself all the time.

Consistent with this, the popular wisdom is that most new year resolutions fail. This is not something on which there is vast amounts of data, but the one survey I saw of two hundred New Yorkers finds that 71 per cent abandon their resolution within a week. I am not the only one.

The good news is that 19 per cent stuck to their resolution after two years. It was not perfect – they 'fell off the wagon' fourteen times on an average. But in some sense, that is also good news – it shows that they had enough wisdom to not give up when they failed, to not use the failure as an excuse to abandon the whole project, and to not give up by telling themselves that it was too hard and would never work. A clear Lakshmana Rekha – say, 'no more sugary drinks' – is important, but only so that the violations remain salient. But once the failure is recognized, it serves little to dwell on it. It is best to move on and try again, resisting the temptation to place oneself at the centre of some epic battle against temptation.

The other important lesson is that commitments are easier to discharge when they come with a little sweetener. Our research on why parents in India often fail to fully vaccinate their children has a lot in common with the dual-self problem. One self knows that it needs to be done. The other suggests that it could wait till tomorrow, especially since there is housework to be done, and your child will surely scream her head off when she sees the needle. But a promise of a small gift when they show up to the vaccination camp alters that calculus entirely. There is something to look forward to right now, not just the stress of finishing cooking in time and the unpleasantness of a mewling child in exchange for some future benefit. We find that this can more than double the vaccination rates.

Perhaps the right strategy for that difficult moment in front of the store that sells the delicious chocolate cake or the very tempting big bottle of Coke, is to promise oneself something small but very nice upon reaching home – like a small piece of dark chocolate, a bite of aam papad rolled in delicious churan, or a fragment of a freshly made kanchagolla with gur still seeping out of it.

The more general point is that commitments work best when they are not entirely divorced from pleasure. A diet is only sustainable if it is inviting, even if the excitement comes in a small packet. It is convenient that so many of the most potent flavouring agents – alliums, herbs, spices, chillies of all kinds, ginger, galangal and their ilk, anchovies, fish sauce and soya sauce – are extremely light on calories. It is true that some of them need a bit of oil to make them pop, but we are talking a tablespoon or two, not a whole jug.

Unfortunately, even when one has a great plan and a heart set on it, life often has other ideas. I was all set to contribute to my inadequate butt with a long list of delicious food ideas (including the recipe below), when I quickly discovered that even the simplest snack food takes much more time than a store-bought protein bar and there was just not enough slack in my day. There were things I could sacrifice – playing less with my children and talking less with my friends – but I couldn't see a way to make that stick for more than a few days. In the end, I feel, except in extreme cases (where the problem is life-threatening), the commitments we make must fit the lives we want to live and not the other way around. Which means they need to be chosen with a realistic sense of our aspirations and limitations – it is best to avoid, as someone I know once did, trying to quit smoking while mending relations with an irate ex-wife.

The Maharashtrian millet bread, thalipeeth, is one of my favourite foods for a healthy breakfast or snack. Serve with a spicy akoori or a dry fried chicken keema, replete with ginger and chaat masala, or just eat on the go, as I do, as an open-faced sandwich, with some generously spread achar that has a bit of sweet in it, like the Sri Lankan 'pickled' eggplant. If you want extra heft in the sandwich, the dry mung dal suggested below works well as a layer above the pickle.

THALIPEETH

¾ CUP JOWAR FLOUR

¼ CUP BAJRA FLOUR

¼ CUP WHEAT FLOUR

¼ CUP BESAN

¼ CUP RICE FLOUR

½ CUP CHOPPED ONIONS

¼ CUP CHOPPED CILANTRO

1 GREEN CHILLI (THINLY SLICED)

1½ TSP OIL

1 TBSP SESAME SEEDS

½ TSP CUMIN POWDER

½ TSP CORIANDER POWDER

½ TSP AAMCHUR POWDER

½ TSP SALT

⅓ TSP CAROM SEEDS

▶ In a large bowl, mix together ¾ cup jowar flour, ¼ cup bajra flour, ¼ cup wheat flour, ¼ cup besan and ¼ cup rice flour with ⅓ tsp carom seeds, 1 tbsp sesame seeds, ½ tsp cumin powder, ½ tsp coriander powder, ½ tsp aamchur powder, ½ cup finely chopped onions, ¼ cup finely chopped cilantro, 1 long green chilli (sliced ultra-thin) and ½ tsp salt. To begin with, add ½ cup of water to this mixture and then slowly keep adding more (up to 1 cup, partly depending on atmospheric humidity) until it comes together into a firm but pliable dough. Make balls out of the dough (slightly bigger than a table tennis ball) and press it by hand on a butter wrapping paper (or any other greased paper) until it forms a disk roughly the thickness of your ear lobes.

Place it on a preheated, lightly greased tawa, hot enough for you to feel the heat rising from it from an inch above. Place the disk on to the tawa and then peel the butter wrapping paper off carefully. Drizzle 1½ tsp oil all around the disk. Slide the spatula under the disk to make sure it does not stick to the tawa or burn. Cook for 3 minutes on each side. Tear off a piece from the side to check if the thalipeeth is cooked well on the inside. Once done, remove from the heat.

SRILANKAN 'PICKLED' EGGPLANT

500 GM EGGPLANT

250 GM PEELED SMALL ONIONS OR SHALLOTS

3 TBSP RED WINE OR MALT VINEGAR

⅓ CUP OIL

2 TBSP SUGAR

1½ TBSP GINGER–GARLIC PASTE

1 TBSP MUSTARD PASTE

1 TSP TURMERIC

1 TSP CORIANDER POWDER

1 TSP SALT

1 SLIT GREEN CHILLI

¼ TSP CHILLI POWDER

A SPRIG OF CURRY LEAVES

 ▶ Cut 500 gm of eggplant into strips the size of your index finger. Marinate them in 1 tsp salt and 1 tsp turmeric for 20 minutes. Shallow fry them in oil that is enough to prevent them from burning. Remove them from the pan and place on kitchen towels to drain the excess oil.

Fry 250 gm of peeled small onions or shallots (cut into the size of the top phalange of your thumb) in the same oil till they start turning brown on the outside. Add 1 slit green chilli and fry for a minute. Fish out the vegetables using a slotted spoon and place them on kitchen towels to drain the excess oil. In another pan, heat 1½ tbsp of oil and add a few curry leaves. Then add 1½ tbsp ginger–garlic paste, 1 tbsp mustard paste, 1 tsp coriander powder, ¼ tsp chilli powder and fry for 2 minutes. Add 3 tbsp of red wine (or malt vinegar) and 2 tbsp sugar to the pan, and mix till the sugar dissolves. Add the vegetables back in and mix well. Take the mixture off the heat and let it sit for 2 hours before serving.

DRY GREEN MUNG DAL

1 CUP GREEN MUNG DAL (WASHED)

1 CUP ONIONS (THINLY SLICED)

½ CUP CHOPPED CILANTRO

4 TBSP OIL

1½ TBSP LEMON JUICE (OR TO TASTE)

1½ TSP CORIANDER POWDER

1½ TSP SALT

1 TSP CUMIN SEEDS

1 TSP PAPRIKA

½ TSP TURMERIC

1 SLICED GREEN CHILLI

A PINCH OF SUGAR

A PINCH OF HING

 ▶ Add 3 cups of water and 1 tsp salt to 1 cup of green mung dal. Bring to a boil. Take it off the heat as soon as it boils, cover and set aside for 30 minutes. After 30 minutes, bring it to a boil and let it took for 10 minutes – the dal should now be fully cooked but firm-ish. Drain the excess water.

In the meantime, in a frying pan, heat 4 tbsp of oil and add 1 cup of thinly sliced onions, a pinch of sugar and a pinch of salt. Fry till the onions turn nice and red but not too burnt. Remove from oil with a slotted spoon and place on a kitchen towel; set aside.

Retain 1½ tbsp of oil in the frying pan and drain out the remaining. To this oil, add 1 tsp cumin seeds, a pinch of hing, the cooked and drained dal, 1½ tsp coriander powder, 1 tsp paprika and ½ tsp turmeric. Mix well and let it cook for a few minutes. Remove from heat and mix in ½ cup chopped cilantro, 1½ tbsp lemon juice (or to taste), 1 sliced fresh green chilli and the fried onions from before, and serve hot.

Energy-Efficient Eating

The world is facing an energy crisis, partly driven by Putin's war, but only partly, since the path to minimize the climate crisis demands that we all use less energy. And one sphere where we can help is by changing the way we eat. Consuming less meat and eating local are ways that are often highlighted, but cooking is another important one, with a carbon footprint of 500 million tonnes a year – only slightly below the 800 million contributed by the transportation of food.

Energy-efficient cooking came up often in my childhood, for an entirely different reason. Foreign exchange was scarce in those days and Organization of the Petroleum Exporting Countries (OPEC) had just boosted oil prices. Imported cooking gas was being rationed: when our assigned cylinder ran out of gas, the cook would put on a glum face, my mother would talk darkly about wasting gas and someone would run to the Indane store to apply for the next one, which could take several days.

On days when the gas was gone, cooking had a very different shape. Each family had its small kerosene stove and a small bottle of kerosene stored up to last until the gasman showed up. Ambitions needed to be scaled down.

But this was a Bengali family; anything below four courses would invite groans and grumpy faces. The cook would quietly announce 'bhaté bhat' – a meal of boiled foods, all cooked together in the same pot with the rice.

I must confess that I was always delighted by this enforced diversion. For one, it was an opportunity to pull out all the pickles, since the dishes were supposedly too bland. Some dried mango (amshi) cured with a paste redolent in fennel and nigella seeds, fat red chillies stuffed with dark matter, thin green ones dressed in ground mustard and the wonderful rosogollar achar (rasgulla pickle) – whole yellow limes pickled sweet and spicy.

And each bhaté, each mash made from something that had been boiled with the rice, would come with its own promise: the boiled potato, perhaps, will get a lift from chopped tomatoes, cilantro, onions, chillies and mustard oil. For the boiled masur dal, it was chopped onions and lemon juice, and a dressing of ghee and spices. The steamed spinach may get something very different – perhaps toasted coconut and garlic. And so on.

Throw in some home-made yogurt, flavoured with a dribble of date syrup (what Bengalis call 'poira gur'), and you have a wonderful meal and the satisfaction of having made the kerosene last another day.

The point, of course, is not that we should live our lives on boiled potatoes and rice cooked on a kerosene stove. Neither the climate scientists nor our dieticians would want that, for similar reasons: both burn too quickly, and neither our bodies nor the earth can afford that anymore.

On the other hand, the idea that a scrumptious meal can be produced on a small stove within an hour opens up an exciting possibility for the lucky few who can still afford to not pay attention to energy costs. After all, the difference between a satisfyingly difficult hike and a painfully steep walk lies mostly in our attitude, in whether we wanted the challenge to begin with or not. If we accept to join the sport of how to cook well with (say) two-thirds the energy, we can (probably) do it and feel good about that. It will require planning the pasta so that the cauliflower or broccoli rabe (that go into the sauce) get parboiled in the water being heated for the pasta, and organizing the menu so that mutton curry can cook in the oven next to the roasting eggplant and the oven-fried Brussels sprouts. Using the pressure cooker to cook the dal, with a couple of extra containers inserted to simultaneously steam the eggplant and cook the already spiced and briefly stir-fried flat beans (sem), might save up to 70 per cent of the energy used for cooking.

And for those nights when you could really do with a little bit of comforting – before that 'casual coffee with your boss' or after an urgent email from your child's headteacher – why not a bhaté bhat? For those who feel that this is drifting too far into the unhip, especially my fellow Bongs, this is my attempt to stake out a piece of the cool for this modest meal. I am sure you can do better. The rules are that you start with boiled vegetables, eggs, dal, etc. Ideally boil them with the rice, but there is no cause to be religious about it; if it can be done quickly in the microwave, so be it. Then play with the mix-ins: chopped onions, cilantro, chillies, ginger, peanuts, etc., and the different oils – mustard is traditional, but why not toasted sesame, peanut or olive? Cooked mix-ins (toasted coconut, say) are fine, but the cooking should be quick. And keep innovating; I dream of the day when I will be offered the perfect parsnip bhaté with butter infused with horseradish, and mashed artichoke hearts dressed with olive oil and lemon.

BHATÉ BHAT

1 CUP RICE

6 EGGS

250 GM SWEET POTATO

250 GM STEMMED AMARANTH LEAVES

250 GM FLAT BEANS (SEM)

100 GM FIRM, SWEET GRAPES

100 GM WALNUTS

1 CUP FINELY CHOPPED TOMATO

1 CUP FINELY CHOPPED ONION (OR SHALLOTS)

1 TBSP FINELY CHOPPED GINGER

3 TBSP FINELY CHOPPED CILANTRO

2 TBSP MUSTARD OIL

1½ TBSP OLIVE OIL

1 TBSP LEMON JUICE

1 TBSP COCONUT OIL

1 TBSP HOMEMADE MUSTARD PASTE

3 GREEN CHILLIES

3 TBSP FRESHLY GROUND COCONUT

3 TSP SALT

1 TSP MUSTARD SEEDS

½ TSP DEGGI MIRCH

½ TSP KALONJI

¼ TSP OIL FROM A PICKLE

CURRY LEAVES

A PINCH OF HING

▶ Wash 250 gm of sweet potato, peeled and chopped into 1" cubes, and place in a closed metal container with 1 cup of water and ½ tsp salt. In a steamer basket, place 250 gm of washed and stemmed amaranth leaves. In a large 8-quart pot, bring 3 cups of water to boil, and place the steamer basket in it on a trivet and cover. After 5 minutes, remove the leaves and set aside. Add 5 more cups of water to the pot and drop in the metal container with the sweet potato, bringing it to a boil.

Add 1 cup of rice and cook for 13 minutes. Then add 6 eggs that were already placed in warm water. Break the tips of 250 gm of the sem beans, pull out the strings, and place the beans in another closed metal container with ½ cup of water and ¼ tsp salt. At the 15th minute, drop the sem container into the boiling water, and at the 20th minute, remove the eggs and plunge them into ice water, drain the rice, open the containers and take the vegetables out of the water.

Take out the boiled sweet potatoes and mash them with ½ tsp deggi mirch, 1 tbsp finely chopped ginger, 100 gm firm, sweet grapes (quartered), 100 gm of walnuts (toasted and broken), 1 tbsp lemon juice, 1½ tbsp olive oil and salt (to taste).

For the relish, take 1 cup finely chopped tomatoes, ⅓ cup finely chopped onion, 1 thinly sliced green chilli, 3 tbsp of finely chopped cilantro and salt (to taste). Carefully slice the peeled and boiled eggs and arrange them in concentric circles on a plate. Drizzle ¼ tsp of oil from a lemon or mango pickle on each slice of egg. Drain the excess liquid from the relish and top it over the eggs just before serving.

Once the amaranth leaves have cooled down, gently squeeze out the water from them with your hands. In a small frying pan, heat 1 tbsp coconut oil at medium high, and add 1 tsp mustard seeds to it. When the popping slows down, throw in a pinch of hing and some curry leaves, followed by ¼ cup thinly sliced shallots or finely chopped onion. Cook for 1 minute, and once the shallots soften slightly, add 3 tbsp of freshly ground coconut. Lower the heat to medium and fry for 2 minutes, letting the coconut brown. Mix it into the amaranth leaves with one thinly sliced green chilli and heat the whole mixture in the microwave before serving.

Using your hands or the back of a spoon, mash the sem slightly. In a small frying pan, heat 2 tbsp of mustard oil at medium heat and throw in ½ tsp kalonji and 1 slit green chilli. After 40 seconds, add some homemade mustard paste into the pan. Cook for a minute till the oil separates, and add the sem and salt. Stir well to coat the sem and remove from the heat.

PART II

ECONOMICS AND CULTURE

Introduction

There is a long and important debate in the social sciences on whether economics primarily shapes culture or if it's the other way around. Karl Marx favoured economics. At the risk of caricaturing, for him it was the organization of production that, to a first approximation, determined the culture: feudal production went with a feudal culture, full of rituals and hierarchies; capitalist production created a more transactional cultural style. On the other hand, Max Weber, another great German thinker from later in the nineteenth century, was convinced that it was the culture which came out of Protestantism – with its focus on frugality and accumulation of wealth – that led to capitalism.

It is easy to see why this matters. If culture is no constraint and capitalism comes naturally to everyone, then it is only policies that are in our way to the wonders of free-market capitalism. Marx (it is worth emphasizing, given his reputation) believed that the dynamic force of capitalism must sweep away the vestiges of feudal economics before the glorious march towards socialism can really begin. This is why some free-market economists from the University of Chicago used to call themselves right-wing Marxists (they just didn't want the final step), and why Marxist parties use the word 'feudal' in a particularly pejorative way.

On the other hand, if culture has a certain primacy over economics, the possibilities for radical transformation might be more limited. Unless you have the right set of social norms, it could be harder to successfully implement capitalism.

Both views have their devotees among social scientists. On the one side, there is the fact that most market-driven growth successes are concentrated in Europe, the Anglo-Saxon countries outside Europe (US, Canada, etc.) and East Asia. It is possible to see this as evidence of the advantages of certain cultures, though those more sceptical point to the fact that the 'right' culture is no longer just Protestantism. At some point, to fit the data, Weber's theory had to be extended to include all of Christianity, Judaism and Confucianism. Will Hinduism be next, notwithstanding the cliché of it being other-worldly? Moreover, while South Korea is now often cited as a shining example of a Confucian success story, in the 1960s, there was a lot of anxiety – in Korea and beyond it – about the same Confucianism, and its emphasis on high thinking and scholarly pursuits rather than manual labour and business creation.

This smells like one of those deep but ultimately unanswerable questions, and certainly not one to be resolved between the covers of this thin book. On the other hand, the context of food and eating practices offers a very natural space to discuss the mechanisms through which economics shapes culture and vice versa. For example, it is hard to think of the difference between Chitpavan Brahmin food and Goan food from a few hundred kilometres down the Malabar coast without bringing in caste and religion – in other words, culture. On the other hand, the US's exceptionalism in food – the fact it has the potential to grow great produce and yet has famously bad food, unlike most other such fertile places (like Italy, France, China, India) – is unlikely to be just culture. The bad Boston pizzas are made by immigrants from the pizza paradise of Naples. The piece titled 'Foodscapes and Landscapes' argues that it is economics, resulting from the particular combination of US's geography and the historical patterns of immigration, to be blamed.

Trade and immigration are, of course, very powerful forces shaping diets everywhere. Potatoes came from the new world and remade Polish and Punjabi food. Tomatoes did the same for Italy. Hakka immigrants from China started a process that gave us *Chineej* food (see 'One *Chineej*, Many Chinas') and a similar accident gave Egypt it's so-called national dish, koshari (see 'The Nostalgia Diet'). The English imperialists left, but their cake stayed behind with us – one slightly savoury exception in the pantheon of ultra-sweet Indian desserts, totally indigenized and sold across the country (see 'The Paradox of Cake').

Immigrants also adjust their diets to their new homes, albeit slowly. Food nostalgia is a powerful example of cultural resistance to economic pressures – people buy the foods that they grew up with even when they cost more, as my MIT colleague David Atkin's research shows (discussed in 'Landscapes and Foodscapes').

If economics changes culture, cultural and social practices undergird the economy; there is now a growing emphasis within economics on the role of social networks in making possible a range of economic transactions, from supply chains to credit to mutual insurance. We need to trust people and we need them to trust us for most economic exchanges to happen. My own research suggests, however, that these networks are not necessarily products of some economic engineering: we thankfully don't make friends only because they will serve some economic function, or pick our family because they offer some economic advantages. We are, with prominent exceptions, first human and then economic agents. Therefore, it is the way we are brought up, the way we relate to people and the way we collectively react to what, within our culture, is seen as egregiously selfish and/or amoral conduct, which make certain transactions possible and others not. 'Trust and Trade' discusses the hundi system of financial transfers that has linked the rest of the world to India for many centuries, and the role of trust in it.

Trust is easier when we know people – we obviously don't trust everyone we know, but a lot of those we trust are people we know or friends of people we know. Social isolation – between different castes who live in different hamlets within the village or between different religious groups who live in different neighbourhoods – undermines trust. That makes it harder to act cohesively on economic opportunities, and also when there is a fight or a standoff. For many years, Ramzan was seen as an opportunity to cross the barriers and reinforce those cross-community connections, but that seems to be less and less prevalent, which is worrying (see 'Breaking Roza, Building Bonds').

Gift-giving is another pretext to reinforce ties, and Christmas (back to the English cake), Ramzan and Durga Puja are all occasions when giving and accepting gifts is socially approved and even encouraged, unlike at other times when we feel slightly awkward in doing so. There is a literature in economics asking why such occasions exist, given that it is easier to send people money than to give them gifts. This seems completely backwards, since the point of the gift is precisely not the transfer, but the fact that both the parties give and take (not necessarily commensurating amounts) and, by doing so, signal that they are open to each other for further interactions, economic or otherwise ('Why Give Gifts' discusses this).

The final piece in this section ('Thrift and Indulgence') returns to the idea of a two-way interplay between economics and culture. Bengali culture, as the cliché goes, is more devoted to eating and travelling than to making money, in contrast particularly with the culture of the immigrants from western India, long settled in Bengal. There are potential historical roots to this divergence – for example, the British systematically undermined the early nineteenth-century boom in Bengali-run businesses. Also, these communities came to Bengal precisely to do business. And in any case, today, most Bengali would-be entrepreneurs suffer from not having other entrepreneurs to learn and get loans from, unlike, for example, the Gujaratis and Marwaris in Bengal. So, it is equally harder for them to succeed in business. Perhaps, for that reason, it is 'economically and psychologically rational' for Bengalis to embrace the eating and travelling that their modest incomes permit than to chafe about not making more money.

For me, despite the very abstract framing, the economics-versus-culture debate is important because it gets us to try and be more thoughtful about all the customs and stereotypes that we lean on in our everyday lives. It won't rid us of all our prejudices – I still can't pretend that I love American food – but it doesn't hurt to fight with them a bit more.

Why Give Gifts?

My great-great-grandfather is one of the figures that most families probably have (or need to invent): whose impractical ways lost us our one chance of being really rich. My favourite story from many my grandfather told me about his own grandfather is the one where he was bathing in the local pond when someone brought news that his stepbrother's family just had a son. He was about to head over there in his wet dhoti (this was before Speedo) when the messenger reminded him that he had not been rewarded for delivering the good news. He apparently hesitated for a few seconds before taking the dhoti off and gave it to the messenger, and went off to congratulate the lucky family. In the buff.

I often think of this story from the point of view of the recipient. Was he happy receiving the wet and probably much-used dhoti? Would he have preferred to wait and get some money? Was he delighted by the flourish of that gesture, or slightly embarrassed by it, or both?

This gets to the heart of the economics of gift-giving: why do we take the trouble to give gifts? Why not just send the equivalent amount by Venmo? Tagore, perceptive as always, framed this issue beautifully in a poem that we read as kids: it is Durga Puja season and two brothers are pestering their mom to see their puja clothes. When she shows them their clothes, one gets very upset – he was expecting something nicer – but as she explains, they just don't have the money. The other, perhaps in reaction, says he loves the gift. The upset child runs off to the local magnate's house, which is being readied for the pujo. People are milling around; some, no doubt, are making themselves useful while others, I suspect, are in the quite reasonable expectation that – this being Bengal – there would be some mishti (sweets) available soon. In my imagination, someone comes around with a large thali of chanaboras, dark and glistening with ghee and syrup.

The boy in the poem looks so crestfallen that, amidst all this merry-making and mêlée, he still gets noticed. The host very graciously gifts him the satin shirt that he wants. But when he proudly comes home wearing it, his mother disdains it.

Re-reading 'Pujar Saj' now, I don't think Tagore wanted us to be upset that the boy begged for it. Begging, after all, has a different status in Hindu culture than, say, in Protestant countries – sanyasis are meant to live by begging – there is no shame in it. It was rather the fact that the boy ignored what it meant to the giver – as his mother says in the poem, he didn't think of what his father had to do to afford even those cheap clothes that year when the crops had failed, whereas for the rich man, it really meant nothing to give away a satin shirt.

There is a 1993 piece, famous in our small world of economists, called the 'The Deadweight Loss of Christmas' by Joel Waldfogel,[4] who was then a young professor at Yale. He asked his students to tell him the market price of the gifts they got for Christmas and the value they put on them, and concluded that just during Christmas, between 4 and 13 billion dollars were 'wasted' because the recipients did not like the gifts they were given.

What Professor Waldfogel did not ask is what those who didn't like their gifts would have thought if their grandparents had handed them cash instead? Would they wonder why it was different this year, if their visible lack of enthusiasm about last year's (entirely unsuitable) sweater had something to do with this? Would it bother them?

In Waldfogel's data, grandparents were, in fact, more likely to give cash (or gift cards). Partly because it was harder for them to go shopping, but undoubtedly some of it was a recognition of their past failures. On the other hand, none of the significant others in his data gave cash gifts. This is telling – some grandparents may have given up on trying, but a lover cannot afford to.

We give gifts to signal that we care; that we thought of the person, about what they would like and the way their face would light up when they realize that someone had thought hard about their preferences. Economists recognize that sending the right signal is important, say when you want a job or have something to sell. But when we think of how we build and maintain our social connections, our instinct is to think about them in terms of personal likes and dislikes rather than seeing them as central strategic elements of our economic lives – as these would be perceived by an anthropologist. Hence, we focus on the happiness from possessing the gifted object rather than on what the act of gifting does to our relationship. Which is how Christmas becomes a dead loss.

As the great French anthropologist Marcel Mauss reminded us in his wonderful essay in *The Gift*,[5] we are always exchanging gifts, be it just an unexpected smile or a few kind words. While visiting friends or family in my youth, there was always a moment for the question: '*Ektu mishti mukh kore jabi na baba?*' (Won't you sweeten your mouth before you go?). It could be something very little, a batasha (a small lump of sugar) or a rewdi (an eyeball-sized lump of sesame seeds held together by sugar), but we knew better than to say no. The social account, as Mauss explains it, needs to stay open – there needs to be the easy possibility of another round of exchange in the future. Maybe the next time you will bring her a letter that went to the wrong flat, and she will invite you to sit for a few minutes and (mostly) lie about how school is going. Then the mishti, which you accept with a smile, hiding well the fact that you are a mishti-snob who only likes the soft and less-sugary kind, but perhaps also noting that inflation is probably eating into her pension and that she seems very lonely.

The point of the everyday gift is to make the more essential exchanges possible: maybe on one particular occasion, the misdelivered letter was actually important; the easy mutual connection, the fact that you would not think twice about coming over unasked, makes that transaction so much easier. This is why the quotidian gift needs to be small – just a token, a reiteration of your connection and one that allows easy reciprocation (a few minutes of chit-chat, a mishti in recompense), one so effortless that people mostly notice only when it's not honoured, when that last-moment mishti is turned down without an elaborate excuse (my stomach really hurts, the next time I'll have two).

Occasions like Durga Puja (or Christmas or Eid) are special because we are allowed to break the everyday rules of gifting and offer something potentially exciting for the receiver. This offers us a chance, as the giver, to express ourselves. For that reason, it does not demand reciprocation: your rich grandpa might buy you that suit that you need for the next job interview, while you might just make him a beautiful card with a picture of your mum.

In a way, that is also how it works with prasad, the thali of mishti that you offer Ma Durga and take home blessed. She, after all, is all-powerful – there is nothing that she needs or lacks. By taking the mishti back and distributing them to your loved ones, you offer her the only gift you can – the acknowledgment of her grace and presence in your life. And maybe that is also why the bhog, the meal shared with the whole community, matters to her. Perhaps, looking down, it pleases her to see that despite all our differences (which probably make her sad), for these four or five days, we, her children, manage to act as a family; that some of the more affluent among us take the burden of supplying banana leaves full of khichuri (khichdi), beguni (batter-fried eggplant), chorchori (sweet potatoes, spinach, eggplant, drumsticks and other seasonal vegetables cooked in their mutual juices into a spicy paste), tomator chutney (as you may have guessed, fresh chutney made from tomatoes) and much else. That, for these few days, those who never cross paths will sit together and be served, perhaps, by those who are more used to being served than serving. That, as we surreptitiously glance at the person across the aisle, we may notice in them the markers of our shared humanity.

I remember loving Durga Pujor bhog, though it's been years since I had some. The one thing I don't love is what Bengalis call 'sujir halwa', often dessert for one of the lesser meals. The Maharashtrian equivalent, sheera, is richer, fattier and better. It's my Marathi mother's gift to our home cooking. Here it is, a gift for the readers.

For the book, I added another recipe that scales very well and is a cinch to make: date and tahini balls. It has the additional advantage of being as healthy as a dessert can be.

SHEERA

1 CUP SEMOLINA (SUJI)

⅔ CUPS GHEE

⅔ CUPS SUGAR

1¼ CUPS MILK

⅓ CUP RAISINS

¹⁄₁₀ GM (25 STRANDS) SAFFRON

¼ TSP GREEN CARDAMOM POWDER

⅛ TSP SALT

▶ Soak 25 strands of saffron in 1 tbsp warm water. Also soak ⅓ cup of raisins in warm water. Set both aside for 30 minutes. Mix 1¼ cups of water, 1¼ cups of milk and ⅔ cup of sugar with ⅛ tsp of salt, and bring to a simmer. While this is happening, heat ⅔ cup of ghee in a heavy wok (kadhai) and add 1 cup semolina (suji) in it. Fry at medium low till the semolina is fragrant and begins to turn red. Add the milk mixture, the saffron (with its soaking water) and the raisins (without the soaking water) to the fried semolina, and stir until the liquid is fully absorbed.

Lower the heat as far as possible. Cover and cook, stirring occasionally to prevent the mixture from sticking to the wok. When you see the ghee seeping out from the edges (after about 20 minutes at very low heat), take the wok off the heat and sprinkle ¼ tsp cardamom powder. Mix well before serving.

DATE AND TAHINI BALLS

1½ CUPS PITTED DATES

4 TBSP SESAME SEEDS

3 TBSP TAHINI

½ TSP SALT

 ▶ In a blender, grind together 1½ cups of pitted dates, ½ tsp salt, 2 tbsp of water and 3 tbsp of tahini.

Form bite-sized balls from the mixture and roll them in 4 tbsp of sesame seeds. Date and tahini balls are ready to serve.

Breaking Roza,
Building Bonds

It must have been Ramzan in the year 1980 when we had this great plan of walking from College Street to Zakaria Street in Kolkata to arrive just in time for the sunset and the subsequent revelries. There would be, I knew, sutli kebabs (kebabs so delicate that they need to be held together with a string), slow-stewed nehari served with sweet, saffron-scented sheermal, kulfi-falooda bathed in bright-pink rose syrup . . . At this point in the contemplation, I needed to stop to salivate, but it went on. Biryani, of course – Kolkata style, with eggs and potatoes peeking out from below the pile of rice – and golden shahi tukras (ah, those days when we never had to spare a thought for fat and sugar). And of course, haleem.

Somebody had the bright idea that we should earn our iftar meal by taking a break from eating. No lunch, she insisted. At 10 a.m., with breakfast still jostling in our tummies, we all said yes. By 1 p.m., brought up on the Bengali diet of at least four good meals a day, we started to wonder about the wisdom of our collective decision. By 2:30 p.m., I was in statistics class, trying to ignore the rumbling in my stomach. Our teacher – never one to fight the innate dryness of the material – was juggling many matrices, but all I could think about was the gooey richness of haleem, topped with strips of juicy ginger and fried onions. And the fact that there were still four good hours before we would get to eat.

This is why children from low-income families need school meals if we want them to learn well. My friend Rohini Somanathan from the Delhi School of Economics (DSE), along with Farzana Afridi from Indian Statistical Institute (ISI), New Delhi, and Bidisha Baruah from Indian Institution of Industrial Engineering (IIIE), New Delhi, studied what happened when, in 2009, the Delhi government decided to extend the coverage of the free school meals program to upper primary students (it already covered the lower primary). They tested the kids by giving them mazes to solve (which is a standard way to measure cognition without requiring the subject to read and understand something) and found that their performance improved sharply once they started getting the meals. It's hard, as I learnt that Ramzan day, to focus on anything but food when your stomach is rumbling.

And it is obviously not just about food. It is hard to think of anything else when we are waiting for a diagnosis or an exam result for a loved one or, for that matter, that one WhatsApp message from him or her that might never arrive. Our cognition is a slave to our affective mind.

But for the poor, this can be a double whammy: they are robbed of their ability to think clearly and act decisively precisely when they need it the most – when their entire survival is at stake. This might help us understand why, during the *monga* months of March–April and September–November – when there is no work available in the fields – a large fraction of the poorest families in Rangpur in North-West Bangladesh ends up living on a starvation diet of 1,400 calories a day or less, even though there is work available in the cities. Those who take up the option of finding temporary work in the city can afford a more comfortable 2,200 calories a day for their families. As the fascinating research by Gharad Bryan, Shyamal Chowdhury and Ahmed Mushfiq Mobarak[6] (another set of friends and colleagues from The Abdul Latif Jameel Poverty Action Lab) shows, this remains true even after they – with some encouragement from a local NGO – have successfully navigated one trip to the city and made a bunch more money than they would have not otherwise. They seem frozen in place by the contemplation of what is happening to them.

My training as an economist makes this feel slightly paradoxical, since we are used to assuming that people respond to need. At the same time, as someone who can't help worrying about whether his children would have enough to eat on their one-day school camping trip, it is impossible to really comprehend what it means for a parent to tell a hungry child that there is no food and there won't be much more for several weeks. I suspect this brings with it a sense of overwhelming responsibility that can be quite paralysing.

This is why, even in a market economy, we need systems of mutual aid. Not charity, though that can be important too, but a norm of helping friends and neighbours in need so that the act of asking can be easy, not requiring us to make the hard choice between begging and starving. Most rural communities across the developing world have a version of this – not surprising, given how little control farmers have over weather, pests and the world markets – and data from rural areas shows that consumption does not go down nearly as much as income during bad times, suggesting that the households are getting help from somewhere.

Unfortunately, these forms of social support are far from perfect and tend to break down exactly when the need is the greatest, when everyone else around is also in need, like in Rangpur. This is why we need governments to be ready to intervene. It also helps to be connected to those who are unlikely to be in trouble precisely when we are, for instance, the distant city cousin who will find us a spot to sleep and make some introductions towards a job. The migration literature suggests that those connections can be a powerful inducement to leave home – indeed, when I was growing up, many friends had 'country uncles' who slept in their living rooms and played cricket with us. More than a third of the working men in Rangpur do go to the city during monga. The right connections may be an important part of why they are different.

This is my favourite way to make haleem, courtesy my cousin and foodie extraordinaire, Vineet Shroff. The nehari recipe came from an old friend from Kolkata.

HALEEM

1 KG ONIONS

½ CUP SUNFLOWER OIL (OR ANY NEUTRAL OIL)

1 KG (BONE-IN) MUTTON (GOAT OR LAMB)

¾ CUPS BROKEN WHEAT (DALIA)

½ CUP CASHEWS

½ CUP CHOPPED CORIANDER

½ CUP MINT

2 GREEN CHILLIES

2 TSP BLACK URAD DAL

2 TSP TOOVAR DAL

2 TSP CHANA DAL

2 TSP YELLOW MUNG DAL

2 TSP BASMATI RICE

2½ TBSP GINGER–GARLIC PASTE

6 TBSP GHEE

1 TBSP ROSE PETALS

5 CLOVES

4 GREEN CARDAMOM PODS

1 TSP CARAWAY SEEDS (SHAHI JEERA)

½ TSP ALLSPICE (KABAB CHINI)

2 1" CASSIA BARK/CINNAMON STICKS

2 LARGE BAY LEAVES

1 TSP PEPPERCORN

½ TSP SALT

½ TSP BLACK PEPPER

½ TSP TURMERIC

¾ CUP YOGURT

FOR GARNISH

THIN SLIVERS OF GINGER

FRIED CASHEWS

LEMON WEDGES

CORIANDER LEAVES

MINT LEAVES

 ▶ Slice 1 kg onions into half rings that are approximately ⅕" thick and fry them in ½ cup oil (sunflower or any other neutral oil) till they are reddish brown. Fish the onions out using a slotted spoon and drain them on paper towels. Retain the oil in the pan.

Pressure cook 1 kg of well-cleaned bone-in mutton (ideally with 50 gm extra fat from around the kidneys) with 1 cup water, ⅓ of the fried onions, 1½ tbsp ginger–garlic paste, two 1" pieces of cassia bark/cinnamon, 5 cloves, 4 green cardamom pods, 1 tsp caraway seeds (shahi jeera), ½ tsp allspice (kabab chini), 1 tbsp rose petals, 2 large bay leaves, 1 tsp peppercorn, ½ tsp salt and 4 tbsp ghee for 35 minutes. Cook till the meat is falling off the bones. Separate the pieces of meat from the bones, and strain and save the stock.

In the same pressure cooker, add ¾ cup of broken wheat (dalia), 2 tsp each of black urad dal, toovar dal, chana dal, yellow mung dal and basmati rice,

½ cup cashew nuts, ½ tsp salt and 4 cups of water. Bring to a boil (keeping the cooker uncovered). Cover with a plate and leave off the heat for 30 minutes before pressure cooking for 20 minutes.

The grains should now be ready to mash up. In a blender, put in ⅘ of the cooked mutton and blend to a paste. Take it out. Without washing the bowl, add the grain mixture and blend into another paste. Shred the remaining ⅕ of the meat by hand.

To assemble, heat the reserved oil, adding extra (if required) to cover the pan's surface. When it reaches medium heat, add 1 tbsp ginger–garlic paste. Fry for a minute and then add ⅓ of the saved fried onions, ½ packed cup each of chopped coriander and mint, slivers from 2 green chillies, ½ tsp black pepper and ½ tsp turmeric. Cook for another minute, lower the heat and add ¾ cup beaten yogurt, 1 tbsp at a time, stirring between additions. Add the meat and grain pastes as well as the reserved stock and the shredded meat, stirring well (to blend) and adding water (as required) to achieve the consistency of a thick dal. Drizzle 2 tbsp ghee over the haleem and bring to a boil. Your haleem is ready to serve. Serve in bowls, garnished with thin slivers of ginger, the remaining fried onions, fried cashews, finely chopped coriander, mint leaves and lemon wedges.

PAYA NEHARI

FOR NEHARI MASALA

2 TBSP CORIANDER SEEDS

1 TBSP FENNEL SEEDS

5 GREEN CARDAMOM PODS

5 CLOVES

1" PIECE OF CINNAMON

1 BLACK CARDAMOM POD

2 TSP CUMIN SEEDS

1 TSP TURMERIC POWDER

1 TSP CARAWAY SEEDS

1 TSP PAPRIKA

½ TSP BLACK PEPPER

½ TSP CAYENNE

FOR NEHARI

800 GM OF LAMB SHANKS

500 GM OF LAMB (OR GOAT) TROTTERS

1 CUP SLICED ONIONS

4 TBSP OIL

3 TBSP NEHARI MASALA

3 TBSP WHOLEWHEAT FLOUR (OR BESAN)

1½ TBSP GINGER PASTE

1½ TBSP GARLIC PASTE

1" PIECE OF CINNAMON

1 BLACK CARDAMOM POD

1 BAY LEAF

1 TSP SALT

¼ TSP GROUND MACE

SLIVERED GINGER

CHOPPED CILANTRO

MEAT FROM THE TROTTERS

SLICES OF LIME

 ▶ To make nehari masala, take a small, heavy skillet. Roast a 1" piece of cinnamon, 1 black cardamom pod, 5 green cardamom pods, 5 cloves, ½ tsp black pepper, 2 tbsp of coriander seeds, 1 tbsp fennel seeds, 2 tsp cumin seeds and 1 tsp caraway seeds for 2 minutes at medium high heat. Take this mixture off the heat and let it cool. Now add the roasted spices into a blender with 1 tsp turmeric powder, 1 tsp paprika and ½ tsp cayenne, grinding them into a fine powder.

To make nehari, heat 4 tbsp oil in an open pressure cooker. Add 1 cup of sliced onions and soften them. Throw in 1 black cardamom pod, 1" piece of cinnamon and 1 bay leaf, and fry for a minute to flavour the oil.

Add 1½ tbsp each of ginger paste and garlic paste, and fry for another minute. Then add 500 gm of lamb (or goat) trotters and 800 gm of lamb shanks. Sauté for 5 minutes so that the meat gets nicely coated in the spices and then add 1 tsp salt, 1½ tbsp nehari masala and ¼ tsp ground mace. Add 3 cups of water and pressure cook for 45 minutes (this is an approximation – if you have small shanks from a baby lamb, then 20–25 minutes might be enough). At this point, I prefer to discard the trotters and just keep the shanks. You can also take the meat off the trotters and set them aside for garnish. Also, take out ½ cup of stock, let it cool to room temperature (for about 5 minutes) and whisk in 3 tbsp wholewheat flour (or besan) – avoiding lumps – and 1½ tbsp of nehari masala. Add this mixture back into the pressure cooker along with 2 cups of water. Bring to a boil and then simmer for 10 minutes till the sauce thickens. Garnish with lots of slivered ginger, chopped cilantro, the meat from the trotters and slices of lime (to squeeze in). After you add the lime juice, adjust the salt as per taste and serve hot.

Trust and
Trade

The first thing I notice in Tashkent's celebrated underground, even before the famous murals and ceilings, is a prominently displayed ad for a local university featuring a faculty member who is a Bengali, at least by name.

Tashkent is about the same distance from Delhi as Kolkata, just in a different direction. And despite the rather daunting mountains that come in the way, there has been traffic between South Asia and what is now Uzbekistan for at least the last two millennia (and probably even longer). Anthony Jenkinson, an English explorer who reached the gates of Bukhara in 1557, reported that there were merchants from as far as Bengal, selling their prized white cottons, though in histories of the time, Multani and Shikarpuri traders, both Hindus and Muslims, got mentioned the most. Many Hindus were in finance, a tradition that the Shikarpuris – who moved to India after Partition (from the city of Shikarpur in Sindh) – continued.

A number of domed marketplaces from the sixteenth century have survived in Bukhara. Tourists like me wander through them, looking for gifts to bring home. In their heyday, they were dedicated to specific products: the many-domed Toki-Telpak Furushon was apparently dedicated just to headgear. Next to it is the beautiful Toki-Sarrofon with its mihrab-like entryway and dome topped by a second dome, which used to be where currency got traded. Hindus from India apparently played an important role in that trade. I visualize a raised platform where the trader sat cross-legged, much like it used to be in Burrabazar in Kolkata, with the white sheets that they sat on (an unlikely idea in that dusty and muddy city, I must say) replaced, perhaps, by beautiful Bukhara carpets.

A big part of finance in those days was moving money across space through the hundi system which, despite the best efforts of various governments, still exists all over South Asia. An Indian trader who had a profitable trip to Bukhara would deposit his earnings with someone in the Toki-Sarrofon before undertaking the trip through the Hindu Kush down to the Punjab plains, dodging brigands and the occasional, overly greedy local chieftain. In return, he would get a hundi, a piece of paper that entitles him to that amount in cash (perhaps after some deductions for the service) in Multan (for instance). But he could also use the hundi to directly pay someone, who, in turn, might pay someone else with it. In this way, the hundi could circulate for a while until it got cancelled against a return transaction where someone in India was sending money to Bukhara (or elsewhere in that general area). The sender could be a trader, but it could also be a soldier of fortune returning home – Babar grew up in Fergana in southern Uzbekistan and his army had many Uzbeks.

The imprint of our long-shared history is in the offensive Bengali word for an idiot – 'uzbug' – but also in our shared love of that magnificent dish of rice cooked in a flavoured broth, 'pulao' in Hindi, 'pollo' in Persian, 'plov' in Uzbek. When you are a guest in Uzbekistan, every lunch and dinner veers towards a plov – rice cooked in a meat broth, studded with small pieces of lamb, julienned carrots and the delicious Uzbek black raisins. Indeed, when you are gorging on the wonderful fruits, the dumplings, the salads and the many different eggplant dishes (I loved the rolls made from a thin strip of fried eggplant, stuffed with walnuts, spices and cheese), be warned that there is always, I mean always, plov.

The cliché about Central Asia is that it is the land of the endless steppes inhabited by nomadic horsemen. And indeed, large parts of Kazakhstan used to be like that. But there are also the snowy mountains and barely inhabited high valleys of Kyrgyzstan and Tajikistan, as well as the Uzbek urban civilizations going back more than two millennia, that produced beautiful cities like Samarkand, Bukhara and Khiva. One thing that all of Central Asia shares is plov; there are as many versions of plov as there are cities in the region, but all variants share the same basic ingredients and the idea of being cooked in a *kazan*, a heavy kadhai-like pot. When Uzbeks and Kazakhs living in Moscow or Madrid meet, there is, apparently, much talk of the merits of various competing kazans.

I cannot but wonder how these Hindu traders, many of whom were probably vegetarian (based on the current eating practices in these communities), found their place amidst these unabashedly meat-eating cultures. Long-distance financial transactions cannot happen without a great deal of trust, as we know from the fascinating research by Avner Greif[7] about the (Jewish) Maghribi traders around the Mediterranean and their attempts at character assassination of those who had purportedly taken advantage of that trust. What happens if a soldier shows up at the Toki-Sarrofon with a hundi issued all the way, say, in Jaunpur (where there was a local Uzbek kingdom in Akbar's time) – a couple of thousand dangerous miles away – and gets told that it could not be honoured because the original issuer was not trusted to repay?

Trust is not easy to come by when you are in a foreign country, especially since the hundi traders also acted as moneylenders. There is, in fact, a record of a rant by a certain Mir Muhammad Amin Bukhari in the eighteenth century, accusing Hindu traders in Bukhara of exploiting Muslims. But the rulers of Samarkand and Bukhara protected them, partly out of their own financial compulsions but also presumably because these traders were doing something right.

Much of the trust was undoubtedly built the old-fashioned way, by being there and delivering time after time. That is how it worked in the deals between software firms in South India and their foreign customers in the 1990s, when Esther Duflo and I studied them. These were the early days of the industry, and some suspicion had to be overcome. The new firms did it by accepting the blame for any problems that arose in the course of the contract, whether or not it was their own fault. But as the firm's reputation grew and the buyers got to know them, the buyer was more willing to accept that the problem with the software might have been their own fault and to pay a part of the overrun. With the hundi traders, there might have been something similar – when things went wrong for no fault of theirs, they paid up nonetheless: an investment on their future. But as in many of these things, there was probably also a role for human contact, for connecting a face and a smile to the hundi and the money. A cup of tea together or a plate of the wonderful Uzbek raisins, dried apricots and pistachios. And perhaps there were some – maybe just a few – who had bent enough to the shape of the place to walk over to some nearby eating place, say, in the shadow of the magnificent Kalon Minar, to share a plate of plov.

For this piece, we combine the recipe for the wonderful plov with two other central Asian dishes that deserve to be better known, both from Georgia.

PLOV

FOR PLOV

1.5 KG LAMB SHOULDER (BONE-IN)

1.5 KG CARROTS

1 LARGE ONION

2 CUPS BASMATI RICE

1 CUP SWEET-AND-SOUR RAISINS

½ CUP BARBERRIES (OR ALU BUKHARA)

1 HEAD OF GARLIC

1½ TSP CUMIN SEEDS

1½ TSP SALT

FOR SALAD

500 GM TOMATOES

300 GM CAPSICUM

½ CUP CHOPPED DILL

2 TBSP LEMON JUICE

SLICED GREEN CHILLIES (TO TASTE)

SALT (TO TASTE)

 ▶ For the plov, soak 2 cups of basmati rice in cold water for 2 hours. Cut 1.5 kg of bone-in lamb shoulder into large pieces (about 2½" along the largest dimension and as big in other dimensions as the meat allows) and put it into a pressure cooker with 1 large onion (peeled and cut in half)

and 1 head of garlic with 6 cups of water and ½ tsp salt. Bring to a boil and remove any scum that accumulates on the surface. Put on the lid and cook for 25 minutes at high pressure. Take out the cooked meat and let it cool for 20 minutes.

Remove the bones from the meat, and try to leave the meat more or less intact (so that the pieces are at least 1" in size along the largest dimension) – this is to ensure that the meat does not fall apart as it needs to be cooked again. Add the bones back into the broth with the now-cooked onion and garlic, and let it simmer for about 30 minutes. Strain the broth, and you should end up with around 5 cups of clear stock. Add more water if required.

Peel 1.5 kg of the tastiest carrots you can find. Remove their tops and tips, and julienne them into matchsticks. In a large, covered pot, add half the carrots, followed by half the drained rice, the meat, 1 cup sweet-and-sour raisins, ½ cup barberries (or the same amount of alu bukhara) and then add the rest of the carrots, followed by the rest of the rice. Add 4½ cups of broth with 1½ tsp cumin seeds and 1 tsp salt. Cover with a towel to absorb the rising steam and put the lid on tightly. Cook at medium low heat for 30 minutes or until the rice is done. Add some more broth if the rice is a bit hard at the top.

Serve with a spicy salad made from 500 gm tomatoes (each tomato quartered and then further cut in half), 300 gm capsicum (cored, seeded and sliced into half rings the thickness of a naan), ½ cup chopped dill, 2 tbsp lemon juice, salt and sliced chillies (to taste).

AJAPSANDALI: A GEORGIAN COUSIN OF THE FRENCH RATATOUILLE

3–4 SMALL EGGPLANTS (680 GM)

1 CUP EXTRA-VIRGIN OLIVE OIL

3 TSP KOSHER SALT

2 THIN CARROTS

2 LARGE YELLOW ONIONS (1½ CUPS)

1 CAPSICUM

1 MEDIUM RED OR YELLOW BELLPEPPER

1½ CUP TOMATO PURÉE

½ CUP COARSELY CHOPPED CILANTRO

½ CUP COARSELY CHOPPED PARSLEY LEAVES

10 BASIL LEAVES (TORN)

3 GARLIC CLOVES

½ TSP CAYENNE PEPPER

1 TSP GROUND CORIANDER SEEDS

 ▶ Cut the eggplants in ¾" chunks and salt them with kosher salt. Set them aside for 30 minutes in a colander. Heat ½ cup olive oil in a wok on medium heat and fry the eggplant chunks till cooked through. Fish out the eggplant chunks and either discard the oil or strain it well.

Peel and chop the carrots into ½" pieces; peel and chop the onions coarsely; seed the bell peppers and capsicum, and cut them into ½" × ½" pieces.

In a wok, heat ⅓ cup olive oil (strained or otherwise) at medium low heat and toss in the chopped carrots, onions, capsicum and bell peppers, softening them for 5 minutes. Add the fried eggplant chunks along with 1½ cups of tomato purée (fresh or from a can), ¼ cup each of coarsely chopped cilantro and parsley, 10 basil leaves, 1 tsp ground coriander seeds, ½ tsp cayenne pepper and a pinch of salt. Let it cook at medium low heat for 10 minutes. Add the rest of the herbs and 3 cloves of garlic (mashed into a paste). Let it simmer for 5 more minutes. Serve hot or cold.

GEORGIAN-STYLE FRENCH BEANS (OR ASPARAGUS) WITH WALNUT SAUCE

750 GM THIN FRENCH BEANS/ASPARAGUS

1 CUP TOASTED WALNUTS

4 TBSP WALNUT OIL (OR ANY BLAND OIL)

2 TBSP CHOPPED SWEET ONION

2 TBSP FINELY CHOPPED CILANTRO

1 TBSP CHOPPED PARSLEY

1 TBSP RED WINE VINEGAR

1 TSP GRATED GARLIC

1 TSP BALSAMIC VINEGAR

¾ TSP SWEET PAPRIKA

¼ TSP CAYENNE

A FEW TURNS OF A PEPPER GRINDER

SALT (TO TASTE)

 ▶ Trim 750 gm of thin French beans (or peel the same quantity of thin asparagus) and put them into slightly salted boiling water for 2–4 minutes, depending on how thick they are (if they are the thickness of your middle finger, 4 minutes should be enough; if they are thinner, they should be done sooner). The goal is to cook them just enough to absorb the sauce.

Grind 1 loosely packed cup of slightly toasted walnuts to a coarse paste. Mix with 2 heaped tbsp of chopped sweet onion, 1 heaped tsp grated garlic, 1 tsp balsamic vinegar, 1 tbsp red wine vinegar, ¾ tsp sweet paprika, ¼ tsp cayenne, a few turns of a pepper grinder, 2 heaped tbsp of finely chopped cilantro, 1 heaped tbsp chopped parsley and 4 tbsp of either walnut oil (my preference), olive oil (may be too strong) or some more bland oil (traditional). Mix in salt (to taste), starting with about ¾ tsp.

Coat the cooked asparagus with the dressing and let it sit for at least an hour (ideally 2–3 hours).

The Nostalgia Diet

During my first time in Egypt, some thirty years ago, I tasted something they called koshari, a dish comprising rice and brown lentils with tomato sauce, a garnish of browned onions and, unexpectedly, some macaroni. It was filling, cheap and tasty, with a nice lift from a vinegary chilli sauce. Many years later, back in Cairo, I was talking to an Egyptian colleague about food. He mentioned something he called the national dish of Egypt, which turned out to be koshari. Since koshari sounds a lot like khichdi, another rice and lentils dish, I wondered aloud whether there might be a connection. My colleague was sceptical. Google, as usual, settled it in seconds. Koshari comes from khichdi, a gift from the Indian soldiers stationed in Egypt, probably during the First World War.

Curiously, a few months later, there were news reports that khichdi was to be officially declared as India's national dish. This, perhaps predictably, kicked off a small Twitter-storm involving the advocates of biryani, *ilish macch* and many more. The government eventually declared that this was not the plan, but not before it raised interesting questions about what a national dish could mean, especially given that there are 1.4 billion of us. Is it the dish that gets the largest number of 'votes', which I fear has some risk of ending up being pizza, especially if the voting age is set low enough? Or something more aligned with a nationalist project – the dish that best sells Indian cooking to the world? That's the way to chicken tikka masala, a pale impersonation of chicken butter masala, invented somewhere in the UK.

My instinct is to go in a different direction – to ask about the dish that reminds us the most of having grown up as an Indian. I suspect a lot of us, when asked that question, would end up naming something from the dal–chawal family, be it khichdi, *bisi bele bhat*, rajma chawal or sambhar sadam.

It's been forty years since I came to the West. And yet, there are still days when I wake up from a dream, wondering when the light became so weak and the world turned quite so mute – when homesickness, evoking a home that only exists in my memory, floods over me. My body wants some Bengali-style geeli khichdi: rice, roasted mung dal and whatever vegetables are at hand – the food of monsoon days when shopping is impossible and there is an irresistible urge to bury oneself under a blanket with a juicy novel.

I suspect that this occasional desire to cocoon oneself in a cherished comfort food is very common among immigrants.

Despite what the politicians of the right keep insisting, most people in poor countries don't want to leave their homes unless those homes are burning either from the global heat or from some local conflagration. One reason for this is that unknown places are frightening. Mahesh Shreshtha, a one-time PhD student and friend, wrote his thesis on how potential migrants to the Gulf (and Malaysia) in his native Nepal viewed their prospects. To do this, he interviewed more than 3,300 people at the passport office in Kathmandu, who were there to renew their passport or get a new one. The core finding was that they have a vastly exaggerated sense of the risks: the median new migrant overestimates their chance of dying during their two-year sojourn in one of these foreign locations by a factor of eight. The truth is that just slightly over 1 in every 1,000 migrants will die during their stay abroad, but half the migrants believe that number is more like 11, a good quarter think it is more like 20, and a fair number think it is as high as 150. Strikingly, even those who have already had at least one round-trip (and survived) think the death rate is 6 in every 1,000 and a quarter think it is closer to 18 (the truth, remember, is just over 1).

The new migrants also overestimate how much they will earn. But the gap is small, may be 25 per cent (the return migrants get it spot on). The fears clearly dominate and unsurprisingly, several months later, a large majority of those in Mahesh's sample had not yet left, despite having gone through the trouble and expense of securing a passport.

Part of Mahesh's project was to understand if it was possible to correct these misgivings and thereby encourage more migration. Even the correct (lower) migrant wages were a lot more than what they would make at home, so migrating seemed to make economic sense. He sent messages to a random sample with the true averages, both about earnings and mortality. This did move their beliefs: both predicted earnings and the fear of dying went down. The latter, appropriately, had the effect of boosting migration by 20 per cent or more, confirming that many potential migrants are held back by these forebodings. One reason that effect is not larger, however, is that beliefs don't move very much. Even after Mahesh's messages, the inexperienced would-be-migrant's estimate of the chance of dying away from home was something like six times the truth, while those who had already been away once (or more), completely ignored Mahesh's missives and stuck to their (statistically incorrect) guns.

To me, this unwillingness to accept Mahesh's (official and relatively accurate) numbers suggests that when his interviewees are supposedly reporting their objective risk of dying, they are actually articulating a much broader sense of disquiet, for which death is just the most vivid marker. Foreign countries are frightening, especially if you are going alone, as a guest worker, very much at the mercy of your employer (and his foremen) and moreover, have a limited understanding of what your legal rights might be. What happens if you fall sick or are injured; if your child is sick and you are desperate to come back to see them? What do you do if you are sad; so sad that you cannot get up or move? Is there someone who will come and find you, and help you back on your feet?

Newly arrived workers, we know from the migration literature, try to quickly seek out co-workers or co-residents, or ideally, a friend or a friend of a friend – someone to reach out and hold onto. I imagine them cooking and eating together, these groups of mostly men living without their families. Perhaps a big pot of khichdi, easily shared. Or a filling *maafe*, rich in peanuts and coconut cream, cooked by a friend from Ghana. Or perhaps, one day, a koshari, the hesitant contribution of an Egyptian co-worker. And perhaps that one will stick and become a habit – one day, several years later, back in India or Nepal, in a wave of reverse nostalgia, he will make some koshari for his family and leave them to wonder what was so special about this simple dish.

The food from around the Mediterranean reflects the long history of people's movements in that area. Koshari, as we have noted, started from the Indian khichdi, but ended up including the pasta and sauce that we associate (perhaps ahistorically) with Italy. The barley risotto marries a grain that seems to have been domesticated in Egypt some 8,000 years ago but now popular in Northern Europe, with an Italian idea for cooking rice. Shakshuka is often associated with Israel, but it is, in fact, North African (Tunisian, perhaps) and got brought to Israel by immigrants from North Africa (on Google, you will find the question – 'Is shakshuka Israeli or Palestinian?' and the answer seems to be neither, but both the countries have adopted it happily.)

KOSHARI

2 CUPS RICE

1 CUP DRIED LENTILS (SABUT MASUR DAL)

1.6 KG TOMATOES

1.2 KG ONIONS

300 GM CAPSICUM

250 GM ELBOW MACRONI (OR PASTA OF YOUR CHOICE)

1 KG CANNED COOKED CHICKPEAS

1 GREEN CHILLI

8–10 TBSP OIL

5 TBSP LIME JUICE

4 TBSP GHEE

4 TBSP VINEGAR

2 TBSP TOMATO PASTE

3 TBSP CHOPPED GARLIC

3–4 TSP SALT

3 TSP CUMIN POWDER

1 TSP CORIANDER POWDER

1 TSP KASHMIIRI CHILLI POWDER

1 TSP CHILLI FLAKES

A PINCH OF BLACK PEPPER

A PINCH OF SUGAR

 ▶ Soak 1 cup of lentils (sabut masur dal) and 2 cups of rice separately for at least an hour. Boil 250 gm elbow macaroni (or some mixture of macaroni and spaghetti). In a heavy-bottomed saucepan, heat 8 tbsp oil and fry 600 gm onions (halved and sliced), with a pinch of sugar and ½ tsp salt, till they turn rich brown. Fish out the fried onions carefully and drain them on an absorbent paper. In the same oil, cook 500 gm finely chopped onions at medium low heat, adding 1–2 tbsp oil if needed, till they're translucent and almost melting into the oil. Add the masur dal, 4 cups of water, 1 tsp salt and cook for 25 minutes.

Add the drained rice and cook for another 15 minutes (or till the rice is done), adding more water if required. Simultaneously, submerge 1 kg cooked chickpeas in salted water and simmer for 5 minutes. Drain and sauté in 2 tbsp ghee with 1 tsp cumin powder and 2 tbsp lime juice. Set the chickpeas aside.

While the dal is cooking, add 1 kg tomatoes in a blender with a pinch of salt, and liquefy. In a heavy-bottomed saucepan, heat 2 tbsp ghee, and fry 2 tbsp chopped garlic and 1 tsp chilli flakes for about a minute. Lower the heat and add 4 tbsp vinegar and 2 tbsp tomato paste. Mix the liquids and let them simmer for 30 seconds. Then add the blended tomato and 1 tsp each of ground cumin, ground coriander, ground Kashmiri chilli, salt and a pinch of black pepper. Simmer for 10 minutes.

Finally, grind 600 gm tomatoes in a blender with 300 gm capsicum, 1 green chilli (or more if you like), 1 tsp cumin powder, 1 tsp salt, 3 tbsp chopped onion, 1 tbsp chopped garlic and 3 tbsp lime juice into a fresh tomato–cumin sauce.

To assemble, layer the dal–rice with the macaroni and sprinkle the chickpeas on each layer. Pour the cooked tomato sauce (from step 3) over it and garnish with fried onions.

Serve with the fresh tomato–cumin sauce as a relish, along with some achar.

BARLEY RISOTTO

500 GM ASPARAGUS

2 CUPS CHICKEN BROTH

1½ CUPS PEARL BARLEY

1 CUP FRESH PEAS

1 CUP CHOPPED ONIONS

1 CUP WHITE WINE

1 CUP GRATED PARMESAN (PLUS EXTRA FOR SERVING)

2 GARLIC CLOVES

2 SPRIGS OF THYME (OR ½ TSP DRIED THYME)

4 TBSP BUTTER

2 TBSP MASCARPONE

2 TBSP PINE NUTS

1 TSP SALT

BLACK PEPPER (TO TASTE)

 ▶ Take 500 gm peeled asparagus, cut into 1" pieces (with the spears separated), along with 1 cup fresh peas. Boil 3 cups of water in a saucepan, toss in the chopped asparagus pieces (without the spears) and cook for 4 minutes. Add the spears and the fresh peas, and cook for 2 minutes. Remove the pan from the heat; strain the liquid into a bowl and set aside.

Meanwhile, in a pressure cooker, heat 2 tbsp butter and 1 tbsp olive oil, and add 1 cup chopped onions and 2 chopped garlic cloves. After the onions turn soft, add 1½ cups of pearl barley and coat it in the oil. Add 1 cup white wine. Once the wine is absorbed, add 2 cups of chicken broth, 4 cups of the asparagus' cooking liquid, 2 sprigs of thyme (or ½ tsp dried thyme) and 1 tsp salt to the pressure cooker. Put the lid on and cook at high pressure for 18 minutes. Once the pressure is released, the barley should be cooked and the liquid almost fully absorbed. Add 1 cup grated parmesan, 2 tbsp butter, 2 tbsp mascarpone as well as the cooked asparagus and peas, and mix well. Finally, garnish with grated parmesan cheese, toasted pine nuts and freshly ground black pepper.

RED SHAKSHUKA

400 GM CAN OF TOMATOES

6 EGGS

2 LARGE RED OR YELLOW BELL PEPPERS

1 LARGE ONION

1 BIG TOMATO

5 TBSP OLIVE OIL

2 TSP MINCED GARLIC

1 TSP CUMIN

1 TSP PAPRIKA

1 TSP SALT

PEPPER (TO TASTE)

 ▶ Chop 2 large red or yellow bell peppers, 1 large onion and 1 big tomato into small pieces. In a large frying pan, heat 5 tbsp of olive oil and add the chopped peppers and onions, and cook till they are soft. Add 2 tsp of minced garlic, 1 tsp cumin, 1 tsp paprika along with 1 tsp salt and mix well. Add the chopped tomatoes and cook until they are mushy; then add the canned tomatoes and crush them into the sauce, reducing them till almost all the liquid has evaporated.

Once the vegetables are well cooked, break the eggs over the sauce and sprinkle black pepper on top (as per your taste). Cover and cook for 5 minutes. The eggs should be fully set but the whites should still be soft.

One *Chineej,* Many Chinas

was six when I first tasted Chinese food. Pigeon roast – a plump little bird, rich with what I now know to be the flavours of soy and ginger – in a restaurant called Eros at the edge of Kolkata's crumbling 'New' Market. It was love at first bite. I lobbied to go back, but the inflationary explosion of the 1960s quickly ate into my parents' fixed salaries, and we ate out much less. The restaurant closed, and I never got to verify whether the miracle I remembered was genuine.

Chinese food stayed with me. On the rare occasion when we ate out, it was often Chinese food we'd choose. Hakka chowmein was my favourite – best when rich in chopped cabbage, carrots, French beans and bits of chicken or pork. I loved steamed bhetki, dressed with generous amounts of chopped ginger and scallions in soy-flavoured sauce. And the marvellous chimney soup, (pork?) broth simmering at your table with different vegetables, meats and many types of seafood.

However, by then, the 200-year-old Chinese community in Kolkata was shrinking. From more than 20,000 in the 1950s, it is now a mere couple of thousands. Economic opportunity had brought them to Kolkata when it was a party central for Britain's grand Bengali bonanza. By the 1960s, that party was well over: years of silting left the river too shallow for large, modern ships – Kolkata's port was mostly dead. Time was also running out on the city's nineteenth-century smoke-stack industries. Like Manchester or Mumbai, Kolkata needed to reinvent itself, but bad policy and industrial strife got in the way. For the local Chinese community, it was time to move on, as they had many times before. Hakka, the name of the community that gave us the noodles, actually means guests (or migrants) – they had a long history of moving south from the very north of China.

It probably didn't help that during the Sino-Indian War in 1962, several thousand people of Chinese origin were either deported or imprisoned as enemy nationals, even though they had spent most of their lives in India. Moreover, this was a time when other expatriate Chinese communities, like the ones in Singapore and Hong Kong, were booming and happy to provide invitations to future workers. Indeed, it is interesting to speculate about what might have happened if Kolkata had somehow weathered the storm of the 1960s and 1970s. This was, after all, when the economies of Southeast Asia were getting transformed – Singapore and Hong Kong, of course, but also Thailand and Indonesia. And in all of these places, the local Chinese community played an important role, partly through their connections to the Chinese diaspora in the West, and a bit later, through their networks in Mainland China. Could something similar have happened in Bengal? The Chinese community was already visibly entrepreneurial, with a strong presence in shoemaking, hairdressing and dry-cleaning. Couldn't it have been a launchpad?

As it happened, the Chinatowns emptied and the Chinese-run restaurants closed. But Indians stepped in. Restaurants with vaguely Chinese names opened all over the city, not just near the Chinatowns. It was alleged that Tibetans and Nepalese with 'Chinese features' were drafted to front them.

The cuisine, quite naturally, started to evolve: Indian chefs leaned towards more robust flavours and heavier sauces. The chilli chicken had more chillies, the garlic fried rice was inescapably garlicky and their generous hand with cornstarch made the sauces more akin to a dal or a curry. Somewhat later, they discovered Sichuan's spicier cuisine, open season for red chillies and garlic–ginger–scallion, with a bit of sweet and some vinegar added to the chilli bean sauce base to make it pop even more. Indian–Chinese food had arrived. Indeed, it started to occupy the street corners where prêt-à-porter *Chineej* noodles were prepared on large tawas.

I must confess that I don't love Indian–Chinese food – all too often, the overuse of dark soy, cornstarch, capsicum, honey and/or chilli bean sauce seems to drown every other flavour, and to make things worse, the soy sometimes smells burnt. To me, the best Chinese meals in Kolkata are still the ones, with the much more diverse and delicate flavours, that we get in the Chinatowns. The last time I went – many years ago, during the Lunar New Year – I had wonderful fish dumplings in a seafood broth, and sticky rice with Chinese sausage and pickled mustard greens that came tied up in a leaf. They told me to stay for the dragon float but I was in too much of a hurry.

Acknowledging this makes me uncomfortable. In theory, the use of Chinese ingredients to serve an essentially Indian palate – gobi manchurian, anybody? – is an excellent example of how to do cultural appropriation right. In the minds of the young men (it seems to always be men) who hawk noodles by the roadside, there may, indeed, be no connection between the *Chineej* they cook and our rich and somewhat scary neighbour. It is just a different way to be Indian – an authentic and distinct indigenous cuisine, much as Chino-Cubano and Chifa (Peruvian Chinese) cuisines are. In principle, I want to celebrate that. Just not by eating it.

On the other hand, the reduction of China's magnificent food traditions to *Chineej* mirrors our national sense of China as the hulking monolith in our north, which drives our often-skittish China policy (admittedly, what they do in our borderlands has not helped). As a matter of fact, however, my (inadequate) reading of their history suggests that while the Chinese imperium has always tried to project itself as a magnificent symbol of Han unity, the regions have always pushed back and asserted their independence. In fact, according to the work of historian Ge Jianxiong[8] (from Fudan University) – which I found quoted in a 2023 economics paper by Haiwen Zhou[9] – between

221 BCE and 1911 CE, China, not including the far west and Tibet, was only united 45 per cent of the time.

The same diversity is reflected in their food. The cuisines of China are as different from each other as Bengali is from Tamilian or Punjabi cuisine. And these reflect deep and ancient cultural divides. The food of Beijing is not the food of Guangzhou, which most closely resembles the food of Kolkata's Chinatowns. And neither is anything like what they eat in Sichuan. The north of China grows and eats wheat; in the south, it's more of rice. In the north and west, they eat mutton and goat like us; in the coastal regions, seafood and pork are the dominant sources of animal protein. In Xinjiang, they eat intensely cumin-y shreds of lamb stuffed into a roti; in Inner Mongolia, that same lamb is cooked at the table in a flavoured broth; the crispy lamb that we love in India seems to be inspired by a Beijing dish. In Yunnan (which is about the same distance from Kolkata as Delhi is), unlike in the rest of China, they eat cheese made from milk that resembles paneer, as well as banana flowers – what we Bengalis call 'mocha'.

China might seem to be a homogenous regime dominated by a single autocrat, but that is not how Mr Xi Jinping sees it. He knows that he needs to balance the needs and interests of these different regions – some much richer than the others – with very different histories, cultural leanings and policy priorities. And though he is powerful, he knows that there are great risks involved in stepping too hard on their toes. As seen in late 2022, the COVID-19 lockdowns generated a spate of protests in cities like Shanghai, making the government back down.

This is important because we, in India, tend to imagine that China's main policy obsession is with foreign policy – specifically, provoking its neighbours. In fact, all of that is incidental to its primary challenge, which is to keep its diverse domestic constituents happy enough, especially when the economy is faltering. It may still do things we don't like, but even those are probably directed towards its internal interlocutors. What, to us, looks like a gratuitous show of strength, might paradoxically reflect the relative weakness of the regime and the consequent need to impress the domestic population by throwing their weight around in the neighbourhood.

For the Lunar New Year (10 February 2024), I proposed a nice Chinese meal that you could cook yourself, which reflects well the remarkable diversity of Chinese food and its ability to coax intense flavouring out of relatively few ingredients.

STEAMED BHETKI WITH GINGER AND SCALLIONS

300 GM BHETKI FILLETS

100 GM SCALLIONS (WHITE AND LIGHT GREEN PARTS)

4 TBSP FRESH CORIANDER LEAVES

2 TBSP SUNFLOWER/PEANUT OIL

2 TBSP GINGER

2 TBSP LIGHT SOY SAUCE

¼ TSP SALT

¼ TSP SUGAR

A PINCH OF WHITE PEPPER

▶ Julienne 2 tbsp of ginger, the white and light green parts of 2–4 scallions (about 100 gm) and 4 tbsp of fresh coriander leaves. Next, mix 2 tbsp of light soy sauce with 2 tbsp of warm water, ¼ tsp sugar, ¼ tsp salt and a pinch of white pepper.

Fill water in your wok or pressure cooker up to a depth of 1" and bring to a boil. Put the bhetki fillets side-by-side on a plate that is big enough to fit them (do not pile up the fillets). Place this plate on a trivet in the wok or pressure cooker; cover and let the fillets steam until the fish can be flaked with a butter knife. (A usual fillet of ¼" thickness should take 5 minutes to cook.) If you want to make a larger batch, conduct this step in several pots parallelly.

When the fish is done, drain any remaining liquid from the plate and keep it covered. Heat 2 tbsp of sunflower (or peanut) oil in a small frying pan at medium heat. Add the julienned ginger and after 30 seconds, put in the coriander and scallions. After a minute, add the soy sauce mixture. Let it boil for another minute, and then pour this mixture over the plate(s) of fish.

CAULIFLOWER WITH FERMENTED TOFU

500 GM CAULIFLOWER

3 BLOCKS FERMENTED TOFU

5 CLOVES OF GARLIC

3 TBSP CHICKEN STOCK (OPTIONAL)

3 TBSP PEANUT OIL OR CANOLA OIL

▶ Break the cauliflower into florets and pan-roast them in 2 tbsp oil till they are reddish and cooked through but crunchy. Move the florets to a plate. In the same pan, add 5 smashed cloves of garlic to the remaining oil. Raise the heat to medium high and let them redden a bit (for about 30 seconds). Add the cauliflower florets back into the pan along with 2 tbsp of water (or chicken stock). Cover and cook for 2 minutes. Once the water evaporates, reduce the heat and add 3 blocks (about 60 gm) of mashed, fermented tofu and stir to coat the cauliflower with it. Remove from the heat.

DRY FRIED BEANS

225 GM FRENCH BEANS

½ CUP TOASTED PEANUTS

2 SCALLIONS

6 DRY RED CHILLIES

3 TBSP CHINESE PICKLED MUSTARD GREENS

3 TBSP CANOLA OIL

2 TSP SICHUAN PEPPERCORNS

2 TSP CHOPPED GINGER

2 TSP CHOPPED GARLIC

1 TSP SUGAR

SALT (TO TASTE)

▶ Trim 225 gm beans. Put them on a tray with 1 tbsp canola oil and salt. Put in the oven at 200°C for 15 minutes.

In a wok, heat 2 tbsp oil, and add 2 tsp roasted and ground Sichuan peppercorns as well as 6 dry red chillies. Sauté for 1 minute. Next, add 2 tsp chopped ginger and garlic, 2 chopped scallions, 3 tbsp pickled mustard greens, and fry for a minute. Add the cooked beans and 1 tsp sugar. Finally, add crushed (but not powdered) toasted peanuts and mix well.

COLD TOFU SALAD

300 GM SOFT TOFU

100 GM GREEN PEAS

100 GM FRESH SOYBEAN SEEDS/EDAMAME (OR 100 GM GREEN PEAS)

2 GREEN ONIONS (FINELY CHOPPED)

2 MINCED GARLIC CLOVES

1 RED CHILLI (FINELY CHOPPED)

3 TBSP CILANTRO LEAVES

2 TBSP SESAME OIL

2 TBSP SOY SAUCE

2 TBSP CHINESE BLACK VINEGAR

1 TBSP MINCED GINGER

1 TBSP ROASTED WHITE SESAME SEEDS

1 TBSP ROASTED BLACK SESAME SEEDS

1 TSP SUGAR

 ▶ Place the soft tofu between two kitchen towels and place a heavy pan on it to get rid of the water. After 30 minutes, cut the tofu into ¾" cubes.

Mix 2 tbsp sesame oil, 2 tbsp soy sauce, 1 tbsp water, 2 tbsp black vinegar, 1 finely chopped red chilli, 1 tsp sugar, 2 minced garlic cloves, 1 tbsp minced ginger, 2 finely chopped green onions and 3 tbsp cilantro.

Put the tofu pieces into the sauce made in step 2 and let them sit for 20 minutes. Add fresh soybean seeds or edamame (or green peas, if the former are not available). Garnish with sesame seeds.

The Paradox
of Cake

I t was the day before Christmas. Waiting for a bus in Metiabruz, the decrepit remains of what was once a very prosperous Muslim neighbourhood, I noticed an elderly man in a skull cap sitting on the crumbling sidewalk, selling cakes out of a basket. He had handwritten in Bangla: *Plaam* cake 9 rupees, *Chrishmash* cake 8 rupees. My bus arrived and I never got to ask him what made the *Plaam* cake more special.

I have always treasured that memory as an example of the unique place of Christmas in urban (and perhaps, even rural) Indian culture. Those cakes were clearly not for some cosmopolitan elite from the city's more prosperous areas. They were meant for the local, mostly poor, Muslim population who, with the rest of the city's Hindus, Muslims and the small minority of Christians, were going to celebrate Christmas by eating cake.

Christmas, of course, is many things in India – celebrated with great solemnity through a midnight mass at the cathedrals, with proper global tackiness in every shopping mall around the country (enormous glittery Christmas trees, heaps of palpably synthetic snow, even the occasional Santa Claus, sweaty under his unseasonable costume), and with Christmas turkeys in fancy hotels, but most universally, by eating cake.

But the reach of cake goes well beyond Christmas. Go to the average kirana store in the middle of nowhere and the first thing that strikes you is just how empty it is: a few batteries, pens, light bulbs, some candy, a few bags of chips and other savouries. And cakes, along with their close cousins, biscuits.

We Indians consumed 1.6 lakh tonnes of packaged cake worth roughly 4,000 crore in 2022, and spent about twice the money (almost a billion dollars) on Parle-G. That is close to 100 rupees spent by every man and child, just on packaged cake and Parle-G.

Chips, I understand. Salt and fat, that's a winning combination everywhere. But Parle-G? Or its equally ubiquitous cousin, Marie, the empress of bland? And for that matter, cake? We are not talking about some molten chocolate lava cake, waiting to explode on your spoon, nor a fruit-dense, liquor-soaked Christmas cake, but its very distant cousin – a pale-yellow mound of flour, sugar, shortening, some eggs, a few drops of industrial vanilla essence, bits of preserved orange or lemon peels and a wonderful Indian concoction: maraschino 'cherries' made from karonda. What accounts for its universal appeal in the land of the gulab jamun, the emblem of excess?

Cheap and durable is, of course, a big part of the answer. Five rupees buys very little these days, but a small pack of Parle-G is among them. And when it is 50 degrees in the shade, it might be one of the few things that refuse to wilt.

But that tells us very little about why it is cake and biscuits that we like. Unfortunately, modern economics has tended to shy away from understanding preferences, on the dubious grounds that, otherwise, we would have to deal with the fact that there are racists and other people who have nasty views. Economists pass the buck, instead, to evolutionary biology, which is premised on the idea that we only eat things because they make us stronger or more fecund. There is no place in their theories for the fact that we live in a society with its own expectations and rituals, and that we eat and drink in part to deal with the rest of our lives. We offer mithais on Diwali to connect, to see the smile spread across the child's face as he or she bites into one, but partly also because we seek to avoid that awkward conversation with his or her parents. We overindulge on Christmas because it's been a long year of many ups and downs, and it is nice to finally let go, even if it is just for a day. We fast at Ramzan to feel like a part of the community, especially at a time when everything else might be drifting apart.

With cakes and biscuits, there is always also a reference, ironically or not, to the other way of celebrating – with candles, lights and booze. But there is also a degree of formality and restraint that we associate with our erstwhile colonial masters. Ishwar Gupta, the mid-nineteenth-century Bengali poet, was so struck by the way the 'English new year' was celebrated that he wrote a poem about it in 1852, in which he rhymes 'take, take, take' with 'a hundred cakes'.[10]

And perhaps, it is that contrast with the all-embracing, over-the-top nature of our celebrations that attracts us to the domesticated cake, which is companionable in a way that a gulab jamun can never be. It does not mind if you crumble it gently and nibble the crumbs absentmindedly, there is no risk of it spurting syrup all over your clothes, and it brings pleasure while never being insistent enough to pull your mind away from work or love.

My children won't eat Christmas cake but they love making dessert. I added one of Milan's (Milan goes by Milou) favourite recipes and one of Noemie's (she goes by Mimi). Anita is her close friend. For good measure, I added one of my wife Esther's specialties: a crumble mix that she tweaked over the years till it was perfect.

CHRISTMAS CAKE

4 EGGS

1½ CUPS RUM

250 GM UNSALTED BUTTER

200 GM BLACK AND GOLDEN RAISINS

200 GM ALMOND FLOUR

150 GM BROWN SUGAR (OR STEVIA, TO TASTE)

150 GM CANDIED LEMON/ORANGE PEEL

150 GM WALNUTS

100 GM DATES

100 GM PRUNES

100 GM DRIED FIGS

50 GM REGULAR FLOUR

2 TBSP LEMON/ORANGE ZEST

2 TSP VANILLA ESSENCE

1 TSP BAKING SODA

1 TSP BAKING POWDER

½ TSP SALT

½ TSP GROUND CINNAMON

½ TSP GROUND CLOVES

½ TSP GROUND CARDAMOM

¼ TSP GROUND NUTMEG

¼ TSP BLACK PEPPER

FOR THE CREAM CHEESE FROSTING

300 GM SUGAR

250 GM CREAM CHEESE

125 GM SOFTENED UNSALTED BUTTER

2 TSP LEMON ZEST

¼ TSP SALT

▶ In a large bowl, take 200 gm of black and golden raisins as well as 150 gm of candied lemon or orange peel, 100 gm dates, 100 gm prunes, 100 gm dried figs and 150 gm walnuts – all chopped to the size of raisins (you can change the combination to suit your taste) – and pour 1½ cup of rum over them. Press down on the fruits to ensure they are covered in rum. Cover tightly and set aside for a week (or longer), turning the dry fruits over once a day. This is only for flavouring – none of the alcohol will remain in the cake once it's cooked.

Cream 250 gm of softened unsalted butter with 150 gm of brown sugar (you can use stevia as an alternative). Whisk in 4 eggs and 2 tsp of vanilla essence.

Mix 200 gm almond flour and 50 gm regular flour (or just use 250 gm regular flour if you cannot find almond flour) with 2 tbsp of freshly grated lemon or orange zest, 1 tsp each of baking powder and baking soda, ½ tsp each of salt, ground cinnamon, ground cloves, ground cardamom and ¼ tsp each of ground nutmeg and black pepper.

Drain the fruits from the first step and toss them into the flour mixture, ensuring that they do not clump up. Add this concoction into the butter mixture from the second step. Mix well. The mixture should be quite heavy by now. Pour it into a buttered 9 × 9" baking tin (with the bottom of the tin covered with two sheets of baking paper). Preheat the oven to 200°C and reduce the temperature to 150°C when you put the mixture in.

It should take about 2 hours to bake the cake, but it also depends on the oven (convection helps). Check on the cake from time to time and cover it with an aluminium foil once the top is a nice brown. Insert a toothpick into the cake – if it comes out clean, take the cake out.

If you prefer frosted cakes, you can make a simple cream cheese frosting by creaming together 125 gm softened unsalted butter, 250 gm cream cheese and 300 gm sugar with ¼ tsp salt and 2 tsp lemon zest. Lather this over the cake once it's fully cooled.

However, if you like your cake a little boozier, bake it a week in advance, skip the frosting, 'feed' the cake with 2 tbsp rum every day for that week and keep it wrapped in aluminium foil.

MILOU'S PEAR CAKE

1 PEAR

1 EGG

¼ CUP ALMOND FLOUR

¼ CUP REGULAR FLOUR

¼ CUP SUGAR

3 TBSP BUTTER

¼ TSP BAKING POWDER

FEW DROPS OF VANILLA ESSENCE

A PINCH OF SALT

▶ Peel a pear. Chop its top off and set aside, puréeing the rest of the pear. In a bowl, whisk together 3 tbsp of butter and ¼ cup sugar. Add 1 egg to this mixture and continue whisking. Pour in the pear purée, a few drops of vanilla essence as well as the rest of the dry ingredients and mix well.

Pour this mixture into a small baking tin of 6 × 3". Place the pear head in the middle of the tin and bake at 190°C for about 20 minutes (check with a toothpick if the cake is firm and cooked on the inside since the dough will be quite runny with the pear purée).

MIMI AND ANITA'S PRALINE THUMBPRINT COOKIES

FOR COOKIE DOUGH

250 GM FLOUR

125 GM BUTTER

125 GM SUGAR

1 EGG

1 TSP VANILLA ESSENCE

A PINCH OF SALT

FOR PRALINE CREAM

100 GM DARK CHOCOLATE

55 GM UNSALTED BUTTER

50 GM SKINNED HAZELNUTS

50 ML MILK

4 TBSP SUGAR

 ▶ To make the cookie dough, break 1 egg into a salad bowl and add 125 gm sugar, 1 tsp vanilla essence and a pinch of salt. Mix the ingredients together with a wooden spoon until the mixture starts to whiten. Add 250 gm of flour and mix everything together using your fingers; the dough will have a sandy texture at this point. Add 125 gm butter and knead until you obtain a smooth dough. Shape the dough into a ball. If it seems too fatty and soft, add a little bit more flour. Put the dough in the fridge for 15 minutes and preheat the oven to 180°C. While the dough cools, prepare the praline cream.

To make praline cream, start by toasting 50 gm of skinned hazelnuts in a pan for about 2 minutes. Throw them into a blender with 2 tbsp of sugar and pulse until you get a powder; set the hazelnut powder aside for later. In a double boiler (or a saucepan set in a larger frying pan with water boiling in it), melt 100 gm of dark chocolate along with 25 gm of unsalted butter. Add 50 ml milk, 2 tbsp sugar and 30 gm unsalted butter into the chocolate mixture and mix well. Take this mixture off the heat and mix in the hazelnut powder. Put the whole mixture back on the flame for 2 more minutes, then take it off the heat and let it cool. (This will most likely make extra praline cream, but it's delicious, so save it to eat with other things.)

Now, bring out the cookie dough from the fridge and shape it into 2 tablespoon-sized balls. Place the balls on a baking tray lined with parchment paper, at some distance from each other so that they do not stick to one another when they spread during baking. Flatten the balls with your thumb, leaving an imprint in the middle. Fill the imprints with praline cream. Bake in the oven for 15–20 minutes. Add extra praline cream as per your taste. Enjoy!

ESTHER'S SIGNATURE CRUMBLE

1 KG FRUITS (PLUMS, PEACHES, NECTARINES, BERRIES OR OTHER
JUICY FRUITS OF YOUR CHOICE)

100 GM SALTED BUTTER

¾ CUP ALMOND FLOUR

½ CUP OATS

⅔ CUP FLOUR

4 TBSP SUGAR

3 TBSP BROWN SUGAR (OR MORE TO TASTE)

A HANDFUL OF SLIVERED ALMONDS

▶ Mix together ¾ cup almond flour, ½ cup oats, ¾ cup flour, 3 tbsp brown sugar and the slivered almonds. Add pieces of cold butter and use your fingers to mix the dry ingredients with the butter until you get coarse lumps. This is the crumble topping.

Remove the seeds from the fruits (which have them) and cut all the fruits into ½" pieces. Put the chopped pieces into a large saucepan with 4 tbsp sugar (adjust the quantity of sugar according to the sweetness of the fruits) and cook until they are fully mushy. Pour this into a greased baking dish and layer the crumble topping over it. Bake at 200°C for 20 minutes or until the crumble is golden and the fruit mixture starts bubbling.

Landscapes and Foodscapes

My mother had a book containing recipes from around the world, in which America was, remarkably, represented by 'New England boiled potatoes'. Being from the land where bland is banned, I thought it must be a joke.

Years later, as a student in the US, it crossed me that the author might have been making a point. Famous American dishes, at least in the 1980s, had an unmistakable over-the-top quality. There was pizza, but pizza that you could sink into, like the carpet in a Bollywood set of a rich family home – very different from the sparsely dressed flatbreads I remembered from Italy. There was chilli, a cousin of rajma, but so buried under layers of sour cream, guacamole and grated cheese that one could miss the resemblance. And while there is steak everywhere, America had the 32-ounce steak. Perhaps the proponent of the boiled potato was a protest against this constant urge toward excess.

Great produce usually goes with great cuisines – think of China, France, India, Italy, Mexico or Turkey. The US is an exception. Like India, it is a country where anything will grow, given the right location. And yet, American restaurants are known, the world over, for their bright lights, big plates and great music rather than the exquisite food. High-end restaurants here have improved vastly since the 1980s, but the average ones much less. The problem continues to be the 'more-is-better' approach to cooking: sweet-and-sour is both too sweet and too sour, there is too much meat in the roast beef sandwich; if double chocolate chip cookies are better, why not quadruple?

In this age of fat-shaming and moral one-upmanship about diet and discipline, it is easy to forget just how much a nation's eating practices stem from its history and geography. Within India, my MIT colleague David Atkin's work[11] shows that people eat what grows well in their home geographies, but when they move, they carry with them history in the form of their food habits – Bengalis in Punjab and Maharashtra eat rice, while everyone else is chewing on their rotis or bhakris.

As for the US: among countries with a million and more people, Americans are second in per capita calorie consumption – they consume nearly 300 more daily calories than the average person in France, Germany, Italy and the UK. America struggles with obesity and obesity-related diseases at crisis levels even amidst the relatively privileged white population. Western Europe, from where a lot of the (white) Americans originally came, does not have this problem.

Geography and history are key factors here. Most people in pre-Columbian America lived somewhere between Mexico and Peru. The vast land masses covering present-day US, Canada, Brazil and Argentina, were mostly empty; perhaps just 4 million people lived in the whole of the US (and 3 million in Brazil). We don't exactly know why, but limits on the food supply – there was no plough for one – probably have something to do with this. The early history of modern US (and Brazil) has much to do with the transfer of European agricultural technologies to these relatively under-exploited (and therefore, very productive) geographies, the resulting plenitude and insatiable demand for labour. And hence, both high wages and slavery.

I have written elsewhere about how elated nineteenth-century European immigrants were to discover that everyone in the US ate real meat daily, not just bones and gristle. India, by contrast – though rich in food of every kind – always faced some population pressure, as did China, Italy and Japan. There were always those who had to make the most of very little – hence, minestrone, the wonderful Italian vegetable soup flavoured by tiny morsels of fatback, or bland tofu lifted by a few ounces of ground meat (and some Szechwan chilli paste) into the marvellous mapo tofu, or the infinitely delicate *suralichi ki vadi* (aka khandvi) made from everyday besan and dahi. While abundance obviously makes life easier, this history reminds us that being constrained teaches us to use ingredients purposefully and makes us find ways of turning the mundane into the special. It is probably no accident that the two great cuisines of the Americas come from Peru and Mexico, historically the two most crowded places in the Americas.

Americans (and Brazilians) celebrated plenitude instead and ended up with the 'cuisine of more'. There are, of course, exceptions like the wonderful cuisines of the African diaspora in the southeast of the US and the northeast of Brazil. But perhaps it is no accident that both these alternative traditions owe much to people who were excluded from abundance – slaves and their descendants – and continue to bear its burden.

The easy availability of space also encouraged dispersed living – it is easier for a man to believe that his home is his castle if the neighbour is out of sight. Sadly, that also means that Americans walk very little, which contributes to obesity. A similar pattern is emerging in today's India. While obesity is still low, it has more than doubled between 1998 and 2015. In a country that, till very recently, knew famine and back-breaking farm labour all too well, the urge to eat as much as one wants and use the vehicle parked at home even for the briefest trips makes perfect sense, but we need to be mindful of where that can take us.

These are two wonderful dishes that celebrate the joy of the Northern spring after the long and dreary winters. The emphasis on fresh vegetables is not accidental.

PASTA PRIMAVERA

300 GM PASTA

250 GM CAULIFLOWER

250 GM LONG BEANS

250 GM ASPARAGUS

250 GM CHERRY TOMATOES

1 CUP LIGHT CREAM

1 CUP GRATED PARMESAN CHEESE

1 LEMON

60 GM DRIED PORCINI MUSHROOMS

5 TBSP BUTTER

2 TSP CHOPPED GARLIC

1½ TSP SALT

½ TSP RED CHILLI FLAKES

½ TSP BLACK PEPPER

 ▶ Add 250 gm (each) of at least three of the following vegetables: cauliflower, French beans, peas, zucchini, asparagus (if you can source it locally), sem, long beans, lauki and tindora (during the summer). The idea is to choose fresh vegetables which need little cooking time and can be eaten crisp-tender. Avoid using peppers (since their flavour dominates the dish) and sweet potatoes (because they melt). Peel the vegetables if required and chop them into 1" pieces (or less).

In a saucepan, add 8 cups of water along with 1 tsp salt and bring to a boil. Boil the chopped vegetables one by one for 1–5 minutes, depending on how long it takes for them to become crisp-tender (peeled, thin asparagus takes 1 minute and so does zucchini; French beans take 2 minutes; a fat tindora might take up to 5 minutes). Fish the vegetables out as soon as they're done and plunge them into ice water to maintain their crunch.

In a medium-sized frying pan (10–11"), heat 3 tbsp butter at medium low heat and add 1 tsp finely chopped garlic. After 30 seconds, add the vegetables with ½ tsp each of salt and red chilli flakes (more, if you like it spicy), and sauté for a minute or so. Next, remove the sautéed vegetables into a bowl.

In a medium-sized saucepan, add 2 tbsp of butter at low heat and fry 1 tsp of finely chopped garlic in it for 40 seconds. Add 250 gm of halved cherry tomatoes (or similar-sized pieces of any other relatively firm but ripe tomato). Sauté the tomatoes for 3 minutes, and you will notice the tomato skin loosening slightly and the juices leaking out. Reduce the heat to low and add 1 cup light cream. Then, mix in 1 loosely filled cup of grated parmesan cheese, the zest of a lemon and ½ tsp freshly ground black pepper. Cook for 4–5 minutes; the sauce will turn slightly pink from the tomato juices and reduce by a third in volume. Check for salt and add the vegetables back in. Let them get warmed, and then remove from the heat and cover. Add 300 gm of cooked pasta (of your choice) to the pot. Mix everything together and serve.

If you want to make the dish truly special, soak 60 gm of dried porcini mushrooms in 1 cup boiling water for 20 minutes and then squeeze out the liquid, making sure to strain and save it. Add the mushrooms to the finely-chopped garlic (before adding the tomatoes) and pour in ½ cup of the mushroom-soaking liquid with the cream. Allow it to cook for a few more minutes before adding in the vegetables.

SPRING ASPARAGUS TART

FOR THE DOUGH

2 CUPS FLOUR

120 GM SALTED BUTTER

FOR THE FILLING

500 GM PEELED GREEN ASPARAGUS (USE WHITE ASPARAGUS, IF AVAILABLE)

340 GM GRATED GRUYÈRE, COMTÉ OR EMMENTHALER

½ CUP SOUR CREAM

½ CUP CARAMELIZED ONIONS

¼ CUP BROKEN WALNUT PIECES

1 EGG

PEPPER (TO TASTE) SALT (TO TASTE)

▶ For the dough, put flour and salt into a bowl. Work small chunks of cold butter into the flour to achieve a sandy texture. Add 2 tbsp cold water to gather the mixture gently into a dough. The more water you add, the more elastic it will feel, but the pastry will end up harder.

Cook the asparagus in salted boiling water for 4 minutes (less if very thin).

Roll out the pastry dough to fit a 12 × 8" pie tin. Lightly prick the bottom of the pastry.

Mix ½ cup sour cream with 1 egg, the grated cheese, salt and pepper, and cover the dough with this mixture. Layer the asparagus on the top, and add ½ cup caramelized onions and broken walnuts over it. Grate the pepper over the tart and bake in a preheated oven at 175°C for 25 minutes.

Thrift and Indulgence

The best batata bhaji I ever had was on a train from Hyderabad to Delhi. I had been smelling it since my neighbour got on from Nagpur and placed his towel-wrapped tiffin carrier dangerously close to me. He must have noticed because his first words to me were 'aren't you going to eat?' I said something about eating at the next station. He waved that away and handed me a stack of chapatis and a fist-sized dollop of batata bhaji.

The sabji was delicious – new potatoes gently bathed in onion–garlic flavoured oil, lifted by ultra-fresh curry leaves and slivers of green chilli, slightly sweet and nutty. I started absent-mindedly – mesmerized by just how much a great cook can coax out of the most mundane ingredients – and realized too late that due to my easy hand with the sabji, I would have to chew through several unadorned chapatis. Fortunately, the train stopped just then. I ran out, promising to come back with some nice guavas, and threw the rest of the chapatis under the train, praying that he was not looking. More than forty years later, I can still recall just how stupid that felt.

He was Maharashtrian. I am half Maharashtrian, but brought up in a Bengali eating culture, where the starch is a much more minor player. Bengalis – as the stereotype goes – are extravagant eaters, which is why they never get rich.

There is something to it of course – a 24-hour trip for us involved many tiffin carriers – some filled with delectable dry dum aloo dusted with bhaja moshla, roasted saunf, jeera and methi ground together. Others with melt-in-the mouth shami kebabs with a whiff of nutmeg and mace, along with many, *many* puris made with the right mixture of atta and maida to keep them soft, and of course, mishti, chosen carefully to survive the voyage. We looked down upon the Tamilian families who ate the same curd rice and pickle multiple times – it was only many years later that I discovered the magic of curd rice, the ongoing fermentation that subtly transforms the taste from meal to meal.

There is a long tradition in economics of thinking of wealth as a reward for frugality; the very influential nineteenth-century English theorist, Nassau Senior, made it the centrepiece of his celebration of the wealthy capitalist. In fact, to this day, economists tend to think of the decision to accumulate wealth as a choice between current and future consumption, which creates a certain false symmetry between the rich and the poor. The fact that the rich save a larger proportion of their income then gets ascribed to 'better' preferences/culture.

And yet, think of the mercurial Elon Musk. His pay package from Tesla, which is currently in dispute, is 56 billion dollars. To consume that amount in a year, he would have to spend *150 million dollars a day*, which is more than 1,250 crores in rupees! How does anyone do that? There is no way to get there even by buying expensive houses – when would one have the time to pick out several mansions a day? What choice does such a person have but to organize trips to Mars or invest the money to get even richer (unless they happen to be so hungry for power over others' lives that they blow some billions on Twitter)?

Unlike Mr Musk, most people need to make meaningful choices, but even then, abstinence has to be easier if you are rich enough (like me, for example) to not lack anything essential. When you don't have to decide between, say, the health of your parents and the education of your children. It is true that choosing both and consequently ending up in debt does not serve the poor person in the end, but it does postpone the horrible moment when they have to deny one or the other and still hope to look into their children's eyes.

And even when the choices are not quite so dire, a person trying to save money is constantly bombarded with options that they must resist. A child has to be told that the luminous pink kulfi will need to wait till next week; the chilli pakora calling from across the street has to be left unanswered; dinner will have to be soybeans instead of delicious moth dal until dal prices come down to earth. For a poor person who wants to save, each day is a battlefield – the temptation to give in just this once and indulge in a biryani meal or a nice party for the neighbours must be strong. But when they do give in, it is back to square one. Maybe it is just easier to not even try . . .

For those of us in the middle classes, the choices can still be hard (for instance, can we afford the tuition at an expensive private school?). Yet, there is comfort in knowing that there is some slack, that small indulgences will not upset the big plans; there can be days when it is too hot or busy to cook but that delicious Hyderabadi biryani on Uber Eats won't break the bank.

But even if someone is able to overcome these psychological challenges, the basic economics of saving is also tilted against the poor. The most attractive way to invest your savings is to put them in the stock market (for the really rich, there exists the even more lucrative world of private equity and venture capital), but that's only open to those who have enough money to put in.

For the less affluent, the obvious option is putting the money in the bank, and pressure from the government seems to have made that much easier in India. There are more than 50 crore *jandhan* accounts now, and there is even a significant amount of cash in them. But even if you have an account, for those containing less than Rs 10 lakhs, the interest rate is usually way below the inflation rate. If you are poor, you lose to inflation whatever little you get as interest (and more).

This is probably why real estate and gold, usually in the form of ornaments, loom so large in the savings plans of the average Indian (ever wonder why there is a jewellery store around every corner?). Unfortunately, over the last decade, neither has been a great moneymaker, with returns that have struggled to stay above the inflation rate.

Of course, the fact that it is harder for the poor to save (maybe why they save relatively little) does not rule out a role for culture or preferences. Almost all the Marwari and Gujarati boys at school with us talked of studying commerce and going into business, and most did. Among the Bengalis, many dreamt of being a doctor or an engineer, but most would end up settling for a bank officer's or bureaucrat's job. It is worth saying that this was our generation – today's youth may be more adventurous. Moreover, we were well-educated kids from families that were able to support us till that job arrived. Those less favoured might have had no choice but to start something – a shop or stall – just to survive.

On the other hand, our Gujarati–Marwari friends also came from comfortably-off families. But they went a different way. I am sure social cues played a role here: they heard their parents talking about the cousin who already had a few crores, and quietly resolved to do better. They saved hard, worked long and stressed about whether they were actually making it. We bought fat books to help us prepare for those competitive exams that guarded the way to our desired jobs and wrote bad poetry in our spare time. Because that, too, was what was expected of us.

And these norms have a way of being self-reinforcing. All my western Indian friends knew someone who was in business: a parent or an uncle who would show them the ropes and help them plan their foray, and maybe even fund their startup. We Bengalis knew very few people like that, which made it seem much more foolhardy to go that way.

I don't have the statistics to say this, but I would be surprised if the Gujarati–Marwari contingent did not end up much wealthier than their Bengali classmates. But I also suspect my now sixty-plus-year-old Bengali classmates pay no attention to those potentially discomfiting numbers. Most of them probably had a comfortable enough life, and found their own – probably quite Bengali – way of being happy without thinking too hard about money. They dreamt instead, I imagine, of long holidays with their extended families and friends, extended train trips with many tiffin carriers, shami kebabs and ghugni, sandwiches and sandesh, keema curry and stuffed parathas, quick runs to the pakora sellers or jhalmuri vendors while the train was at the station, antakshari in the evening and silly jokes through the day.

I grew up in an age where people were very mindful of not spending more than they needed to, and foods that travel well was an important part of that story. Here, I suggest three: one vegetarian (interestingly, from Finland), one with fish and one that is meat-based.

SHAMI KEBAB

500 GM KEEMA

150 GM CHANA DAL (SOAKED OVERNIGHT)

½ CUP CILANTRO

¼ CUP MINT

1¼ CUP MINCED ONIONS

2 BAY LEAVES

2 BLACK CARDAMOMS

2 FLAKES OF MACE (JAVITRI)

1" CINNAMON

3½ TBSP MINCED GINGER

2 TBSP MINCED GARLIC

1½ TSP SALT

1½ TSP CUMIN

½ TSP BLACK PEPPER

⅛ TSP NUTMEG 3 GREEN CHILLIES (SLICED)

▶ To a pressure cooker, add the fatty keema, soaked chana dal, ¾ cup of chopped onion, 2 tbsp garlic and 1 tbsp ginger, along with the dry whole spices – cinnamon, bay leaves, black cardamom pods, cumin, freshly ground black pepper, grated nutmeg, mace (javitri) – and 1½ tsp salt. Now, add 1½ cups of water to the mixture.

Lid the pressure cooker and cook for 20 minutes after the first whistle at medium low heat, while ensuring that the cooker does not run out of water. Release the pressure in the cooker and if there is any water left, cook it while open, stirring till it dries fully. Let the mixture cool.

Once cooled, grind the mixture in a food processor for 3 minutes until it's smooth. Now add ½ cup chopped onion, ½ cup chopped cilantro, ¼ cup chopped mint, 2½ tbsp chopped ginger and 3 sliced green chillies (chop these ingredients as finely as possible). Refrigerate this mixture for about 45 minutes or more.

With slightly oiled hands, shape your patties; you should be able to make 15 patties with this mixture. Heat a non-stick pan and slightly drizzle it with oil (about 1 tbsp oil for a 10" pan). Once the pan is slightly hot, shallow-fry the patties for 3 minutes on each side at medium heat. Drizzle drops of extra oil for the patties to crisp up on the outside.

FISH SEEKH KEBAB

500 GM FISH FILLET (SURMAI OR BHETKI, CUT INTO 1" CUBES)

1 CUP YOGURT

2 TBSP CHOPPED CILANTRO

2 TBSP GHEE

1 TBSP GREEN CHILLI PASTE

1 TBSP GINGER–GARLIC PASTE

½ TBSP GARAM MASALA POWDER

1 TSP TURMERIC

1 TSP SALT

▶ Take 500 gm of fillet of a meaty fish (like surmai or bhetki), cut into 1" cubes, and marinate it in a mixture of 1 cup yogurt, 1 tsp turmeric, 1 tsp salt, 1 tbsp ginger–garlic paste, ½ tbsp garam masala powder, 1 tbsp green chilli paste and 2 tbsp of chopped cilantro. Set aside for an hour. Put them on seekhs (skewers) and cook over a hot grill for 6–8 minutes (or under a hot broiler), basting occasionally with 2 tbsp of ghee.

PIRAKKA

1 CUP RYE FLOUR

1 CUP RICE

2 CUPS MILK

½ CUP ALL-PURPOSE FLOUR

1 TSP KALONJI

1 TSP SALT

▶ For the dough, mix 1 cup rye flour, ¼ cup all-purpose flour, ½ tsp salt and ½ cup water. Knead the dough and divide it into ten portions. Roll them into very thin rounds on a floured surface.

For the filling, add 1 cup of rice into a pan with 2 cups of water. Cook the rice till the water evaporates. Then add 2 cups of milk and the kalonji, and cook for 20 minutes at medium low heat till the rice is sticky. Lastly, add ½ tsp salt.

Preheat the oven to 200°C. Put the filling in the middle of the rolled-out dough and fold its edges upward, crimping them together to give the pirakka its shape. Bake for 15 minutes.

PART III

ECONOMICS AND SOCIAL POLICY

Introduction

My first serious exposure to the practice of modern economics was in the 1980s, when the profession was in the middle of a serious lurch to the right. This was the time of Ronald Reagan and Margaret Thatcher, who were telling us that all our economic woes were caused by high taxes and wanton public generosity. Markets work; we just need to let them do their magic by not distorting incentives.

Economists are often sympathetic to this message. Even from my position as a very junior member of the profession, it was hard to miss the way lots of prominent figures in the field were lining up nicely with this political programme, claiming 'evidence' that social security or corporate tax was ruining everything. Any mention of the need to intervene in markets would get the confident riposte: 'Is there really a reason to believe that the market is not doing its job?' Any mention of helping people with their incomes or access to credit and healthcare would predictably get a pushback – how about the disincentive effects?

We now know well what happened. Taxes were cut, welfare was slashed and laws were changed so that trade unions could not do their job of protecting workers' rights. The rich got richer; in data collected by World Inequality Lab (WIL), the concentration of income and wealth at the very top starts rising exactly around 1980 in the UK and the US, coinciding almost uncannily with the rise of these right-wing ideologues.

On the other hand, there is no evidence that all this incentivization (an ugly word that dates, I think, from the same period) did anything good for the slowing growth rate in those countries. With growth remaining slow and a growing share of income going to the super-rich, the median inflation-adjusted hourly earnings of wage and salaried workers in the US were slightly lower in 2016 than in 1979. The experience in the UK was less stark, but the earnings at the bottom of the distribution went up by much less than those at the top. No lines of causality in history are entirely straightforward but it is reasonable to ask whether, without this particular toxic combination of economics and politics, we would have ended up with Brexit and rampant Trumpism.

Economists' obsession with not being 'too nice' to the poor so that they don't become lazy is not new. Prominent British economists in the nineteenth century were keen to ensure that the poor support programmes were appropriately mean and nasty. Inspired by them, famine policy under the British in the late-eighteenth and nineteenth centuries often consisted of doing almost nothing. Many millions died. In 'Lessons from the Imambara', I contrast this with the relatively generous policies of feeding anyone who shows up for work that we see in north India before the takeover. However, though the British have now been gone for almost eighty years, my experience of working with welfare bureaucracies in India suggests that the suspicion of making things too easy for the poor – instilled in us by our erstwhile masters – persists.

That being said, there is a perceptible and welcome shift in the general attitude towards being a bit more generous to the poor. The number of countries where there is some kind of transfer programme for the poor, in cash or in kind, has been growing since the 1990s. In 2020–21, according to the World Bank, there were 962 cash transfer programmes spread across 203 countries covering 1.36 billion people. A lot of these programmes have been studied in detail, and what they show quite uniformly is that getting extra social support does not make people lazy.

If anything, the evidence points in the opposite direction. 'An Income Guarantee' sets out some potential narratives about why this is the case; I imagine a poor woman who dreams of starting a roadside eatery (she has it planned down to the menu she would serve). But it is easy to think of the many reasons why, without a cash transfer, she will not hit launch and why, therefore, once she gets the transfer, she will get super busy.

Not every social problem can, however, be solved by transfers. India is the malnutrition capital of the world, with much more stunting and wasting than much poorer countries in Asia and especially Africa. And even our middle-class children are too small. In 'India's Protein Problem', I argue that the problem is our traditional diet – we just don't eat anywhere near the amount of protein we need, especially when young. We need information campaigns targeted at parents, focusing on proteins. I make a case for including more peanuts in our cooking, perhaps by evolving West African-style peanut stews to suit our palate.

Climate change and the increasing prevalence of super-hot days when being outside for more than a few minutes can be deadly, will require a different type of public intervention. Shelters, where people can rest and cool down when heat-exhaustion hits them (or just anticipating that it will), can save lives. In 'Adapting to Hot Summers', I try to imagine some of these shelters, suggesting that they should have a small kiosk serving healthy cooling drinks and offer some ideas for the same.

A third, necessary direction is in legal reform. The average incarcerated person in India is an under-trial who has been there often for months or even years. He is entitled to bail but, being poor and semi-literate, has no idea how to get there. And in the meanwhile, the prison authorities discriminate against poor inmates in every possible way, down to the kinds of diet they are entitled to. In the piece titled 'Unfair Imprisonments', I write about my own experience in Tihar Jail many decades ago and contrast it with that of another young man who did not have the same social advantages as I did.

The piece on 'Conspicuous Consumption' is even more directly about inequality and how the ability of some to spend almost unlimited amounts may affect others, especially if it is very conspicuous. The piece 'Thoughtful Giving' focuses on the flip side – the potential for philanthropy instead of private consumption. I argue that despite the (very welcome) shift in attitudes against doing anything for the poor, ideology still plays a very important role in what donors want to support. I write – a tad ungenerously perhaps – about the culture of donor gatherings, where the same predictable canapés get served and the same lazy opinions get rehearsed all too often, even though we now have a much more nuanced understanding of most of these questions. And yet, given the ballooning wealth of the super-rich, it is impossible to ignore the power of the donors, and their enormous and growing potential to do good.

'Why I Won't Start a Restaurant' is on the other side of conspicuous consumption – specifically on fine dining. I discuss what it takes to run a restaurant well, and why (to return to a theme that launched this section) it is not really about incentives.

Lessons from the Imambara

When I was growing up, we all knew families that were on their way down financially. Once prosperous or even wealthy, they had been undermined by a generation (or two) of profligacy and self-indulgence. Their impressive houses were falling apart, the latest round of repairs being held up by fights between the brothers ('Who left the tap running in the bathroom?'). The 1950s Austins or Chevrolets still stood on their rusting wheels in the garages, mostly because it was too hard to accept that there would be no more family jaunts. The few old family retainers that remained could recall the daily ten-course dinners for twenty-five in the main dining room. Now the siblings and their families ate separately behind closed doors, perhaps to conceal just how frugal their meals had become.

I thought of those days and those families when I was in Lucknow recently. We decided to visit the Bada Imambara during the two hours before the flight. This is an enormous prayer hall from the 1780s, sponsored by the then Nawab of Awadh, Asaf-ud-Daulah, in response to a terrible drought and the resulting famine. It was a food-for-work programme – anyone who came for work on the building project got some basic provisions.

There is a famous maze inside the Imambara called the 'bhool bhulaiya'. The guide we took to avoid getting lost told us an interesting story about it. Apparently, the local upper classes were also starving – not surprising, given that they, too, lived off the land. The nawab knew that they were too proud to show up for work with the everyday labourers. So, instead, he paid them to come hidden in the dark of the night through the bhool bhulaiya to demolish a part of the day's work.

I am not sure I entirely believe it, but it's a great story. Two interesting points come out of it. First, the nawab wanted people to work for their food. I am no expert, but I don't think of that as an Indian tradition. Sita crossed the Lakshmana Rekha to honour a beggar (Ravana in disguise), even though she was expressly forbidden to do so. She didn't think of what work she was going to ask him to do in return. Bhikkhus and fakirs have a very specific role in Indian religious culture – both Hindu and Muslim families would think twice before turning either away and would certainly never ask them to do something in return. On the other hand, the Rohilla chieftain Hafiz Rahmat Khan was using famine-hit labour for public construction – including the famous Pilibhit mosque – even before 1780. Where did he get the idea?

The second point is that welfare recipients' dignity was important to the nawab. Whether or not I think this is the right priority, the nawab cared about the fact that ashraf mussalmans would rather die than work shoulder-to-shoulder with their own servants – just the way we, as children, knew not to dig too deep when one of our once-prosperous relatives showed up without the gold bangle she always wore and claimed it was lost.

Both these choices – of there being a work requirement and how the beneficiaries should be treated – would become important issues for the British, who, exactly around 1780, assumed the overlordship of large parts of northern India and, therefore, the responsibility for managing the periodic droughts and consequent famines that afflicted the area. Being a private company, the East India Company was mostly dedicated to making money, hence, these issues troubled them a lot. Land revenue was an important part of their earnings, and collections tended to fall during the drought years. They were, therefore, not exactly keen to spend more money to help the starving.

But it was impossible to not do anything either. During the 1783 famine, the fledgling East India Company's administration discovered that many people left their homes in search of work and food, and never came back. Others died. Large areas were depopulated. With no people to work the land, productivity and land revenue crashed.

Moreover, it is hard to get people to pay taxes to a state that seems indifferent to their well-being, and in those early days, the EIC knew that it was being compared with the regimes it displaced (or was trying to displace), like Awadh. Finally, and perhaps equally importantly, on the ground that the company was represented by people – British men and women, often quite young – for whom the starving faces and the piling dead bodies were a daily reality. They could not but want to do something. Fanny Eden, sister of Lord Auckland (the then Governor-General of India), writing during the brutal 1838 famine in Agra, put it bluntly:

'But it is no affection to say that when we sit down to dinner with the band playing and all the pomp and circumstances of life about us, which is just as much kept up in a tent as anywhere else, my very soul sickens at the cries of the starving children outside which never seem to cease.'

I know all this only because one of my dearest friends from my JNU years, Sanjay Sharma, is the author of the seminal book, *Famine, Philanthropy and the Colonial State: North India in the Early Nineteenth Century*.

Sanjay observes that the bottom-up pressure to relieve the misery caused by the famines ran up against the growing influence of laissez-faire thinking in Britain at the time. Indeed, many of the ameliorative efforts by the local (British) administrators got quashed by their higher-ups. This was done, of course, partly because they wanted to conserve money. But there was also a strong ideological element in it, in keeping the contemporary emphasis on 'scientific economic basis' for charity – in contrast with the Indian traditions which placed a value on the idea of giving itself. These were frequently described by British observers as irrational or hypocritical, based on piety and the desire to earn credit in heaven. 'Rational charity', on the other hand, was all about avoiding waste: 'overly generous' policies were frowned upon because they might encourage people to stop working and live off public munificence (they also cost the company more).

The debate on how to ensure that charity was also 'good economics' went on for years. In the meanwhile, there were famines when little was done and many died. It was only during the awful 1838 Agra famine – which Ms Eden was writing about – that a clear policy of providing public employment to the needy, much like in Lucknow and Pilibhit, emerged. However, Fanny Eden's brother, the Governor-General, made sure that these jobs would pay so little that only those who had no choice would take them. And to make it more acceptable to the devotees of economic rationality, the plan was to put the labour to good use: to build irrigation canals that would raise productivity and prevent famines, and roads to move grains to where there was scarcity. In fact, many of these got built.

This only covered those who were able to work. The rest, like women with young children or the handicapped, were left to their fate. It was only after 1861 that the government started building poorhouses, where such people could get some food, after many intense debates about just how little dal–roti could suffice.

None of this prevented the recurrence of murderous famines. Bad weather and blind ideology continued to take their toll. Estimates suggest that 8.2 million people died just in the 1876–78 famine. But for better or for worse, these ideas continue to guide our approach to social transfers. The

Mahatma Gandhi National Rural Employment Guarantee Act (MGNREGA) is modelled exactly on the public works of the earlier periods, though Lord Auckland would have surely thought it is too generous. Perhaps, as a result, it works. Research by Clement Imbert and John Papp[12] shows that it reduces rural poverty.

At the same time, our governments are still all too concerned with ensuring that only the truly desperate – prepared to navigate the bureaucratic mazes and not be discouraged by the many engineered dead ends – get benefits. Getting a widow's pension in Delhi, a study by the World Bank's Sarika Gupta[13] tells us, requires two visits, on average, to the local MLA among the many tedious and/or humiliating steps. As a result, many of the eligible just give up. Our recent work in Tamil Nadu finds something similar. Maybe we should consider relaxing a bit about keeping the undeserving out, so as not to exclude those in real need. And perhaps, even try to be respectful of the beneficiary's humanity; I can picture the nawab sanctioning some mithai (some shahi tukra?) for his workers on the rare *parab* days. I suspect Lord Auckland wouldn't ever do the same.

I imagine a household in famine times – relieved that they had resisted the EIC's push towards cash crops and monocultures, and planted some hardy millets that luckily survived the drought – making a delicious khichdi with whatever little they had: scraps of vegetables, some dal and some peanuts for protein. Here are three variants on that theme, from the west, the south and the east of India. Give me some pickle with any of these, and I am happy.

BAJRA KHICHDI

2 CUPS CAULIFLOWER FLORETS

2 CUPS FROZEN PEAS

1 CUP BAJRA

1 CUP CHOPPED TOMATO

1 CUP YELLOW MUNG DAL

4 TBSP GHEE/OIL

4 GREEN CARDAMOM PODS

2 CLOVES

2 BAY LEAVES

1" PIECE OF CINNAMON

1 TSP CUMIN SEEDS

1 TSP TURMERIC POWDER

½ TSP DEGGI MIRCH

SALT (TO TASTE)

FOR CHHAUNK

4 CRUSHED CLOVES OF GARLIC

A PINCH OF HING

1 DRIED RED CHILLI

½ CUP PEANUTS (OR CASHEW NUTS)

 ▶ In a saucepan, add 1 cup of bajra, 3 cups of water, a pinch of salt and bring to a boil. Turn off the heat and cover. Set aside for 1.5 hours. Drain. In a pressure cooker, heat 2 tbsp of ghee/oil at medium high and add a 1" piece of cinnamon, 4 cardamom pods, 2 cloves, 1 tsp cumin seeds and 2 bay leaves.

After a minute, add 1 cup of yellow mung dal. Reduce the heat to medium and fry till the dal starts to turn red. Add the drained millets, 1 tsp salt, 1 tsp turmeric powder, ½ tsp deggi mirch, 1 cup chopped tomato and 3 cups of water. Put the lid on and cook at high pressure for 8 minutes, and then release the pressure. The bajra and the dal should now be soft, but not yet falling apart. Next, fry 2 cups of cauliflower florets till nicely red. Add these to the khichdi along with 2 cups of frozen peas and 1 cup water. Simmer for 10 minutes.

Fry 4 crushed cloves of garlic in 2 tbsp of ghee/oil along with a pinch of hing and 1 dried red chilli till they turn red. Add ½ cup peanuts (or if you want to be fancy, cashews) and fry for another minute. Pour the chhaunk over the khichdi.

BISI BELE BHAT

1 CUP TOOR DAL

1 CUP RICE

1 CUP COARSELY CHOPPED ONIONS

¾ CUP POTATOES

¾ CUP CARROTS

¾ CUP CABBAGE

¾ CUP CAULIFLOWER

2 TBSP BISI BELE BHAT POWDER (STORE-BOUGHT)

2 TSP TAMARIND PASTE

2 TSP SALT

1 TSP TURMERIC POWDER

FOR CHHAUNK

4 TBSP BROKEN CASHEW NUTS

2 TBSP GHEE

A SPRIG OF CURRY LEAVES

 ▶ Boil 3 cups of water. Take this water off the heat and soak 1 cup toor dal in it for 30 minutes. Put the soaked toor dal into a pressure cooker along with 1 cup rice, 1 tsp salt and 1 tsp turmeric powder. Pressure cook for 10 minutes.

In another pressure cooker, put in the coarsely chopped onions, potatoes, carrots, cabbage and cauliflower. Add 2 cups of water, 2 tbsp store-bought bisi bele bhat powder, 2 tsp tamarind paste and 1 tsp salt. Pressure cook for 10 minutes.

In a large pot, mix the contents of both the pressure cookers and cook on low heat for 10 minutes, uncovered, so that the flavours meld together.

Fry 4 tbsp broken cashew nuts and a sprig of curry leaves in 2 tbsp ghee till the cashew nuts turn golden. Add this chhaunk into the pot of bisi bele bhat and mix well.

KALAI DALER KHICHURI

1 CUP SABUT (WHOLE) URAD DAL

½ CUP GOBINDOBHOG RICE

2 TSP CUMIN SEEDS

2 TSP SALT

2 TSP GRATED GINGER

1 TSP PEPPERCORNS

½ TSP TURMERIC POWDER

FOR CHHAUNK

2 TBSP GHEE

1 BAY LEAF

1 TSP CUMIN

A PINCH OF HING

 ▶ Dry roast 1 cup of sabut urad dal on a skillet for 5 minutes; remove it in a bowl, add water to it and soak overnight. Also soak 1 tsp peppercorns and 2 tsp cumin seeds in 3 tbsp water for 2 hours, and then grind to a paste. Add the overnight-soaked dal to a saucepan with 1 tsp salt and bring to a boil. Reduce the heat and cook till the grains of dal can be mashed between two fingers.

Add ½ cup gobindobhog rice, the cumin–pepper paste, 2 tsp grated ginger, 1 tsp salt and ½ tsp turmeric powder, and cook till the rice is done. For the chhaunk, in a small saucepan, heat 2 tbsp ghee and add 1 bay leaf, 1 tsp cumin seeds and a pinch of hing. Fry for 30 seconds, and pour it over the khichuri and mix well.

An Income Guarantee

I must have been six or seven when, for the first and probably last time, my parents were invited to a new year's eve party where children were also invited. It was in a big house somewhere in Ballygunge, and a whole wing was set aside for children's activities, with several nannies running around. The children's wing had limited success, I must add, because we had heard that a certain maharani would be attending and that was all that we could think about. Our parents, presumably in order to protect the maharani from a gaggle of curious children, refused to identify her. So, we tried it on our own. No one was wearing a crown – the one who came in a tiara was her cousin, a kid assured us, and certainly not the queen. Eventually, each of us made our own picks. Mine was a long-nosed woman in a silver-grey sari, who I heard – in a voice heavily inflected with boredom (that I later came to associate with many years of smoking) – asking a certain (male) 'darling' to get her another gin and tonic.

I think most of us have had the experience of that new year's eve celebration that was so hyped that it was doomed to disappoint. And the one which you already know will not measure up, but you need to go through the motions anyway. I still wonder what it was for my maharani.

Overpromising and underdelivering is, of course, one of the occupational hazards of my world, where the latest innovations in development thinking are subjected to the occasionally brutal test of evidence. The latest on the docket is Universal Basic Income (UBI). The idea that everyone should get a basic minimum income, irrespective of what else is happening in their economic lives, has an appeal to a wide constituency. It ranges from those who believe that there cannot be a moral justification for the kind of extreme poverty we sometimes see in India, to Silicon Valley billionaires worrying about the political fallout from the AI-induced job losses. By making it universal and unconditional, the argument goes, we remove the incentive for people to exaggerate their poverty, say, by working less. The evidence in developing countries suggests that this concern about strategic laziness is overblown but people do try to hide their authentic earnings (by taking cash payments, for example). For that reason, government programs that try to target the poor often end up leaking a significant fraction to the non-poor and perhaps, more regrettably, the (imperfectly implemented) extra checks intended to prevent that leakage often end up excluding a large fraction of the genuinely needy. Universal unconditional programmes avoid these targeting errors, but on the other hand, they only 'solve' the problem by giving money to lots of people who don't need it. This, in turn, lessens the amounts of money the really deserving can receive.

On the other hand, there are many reasons why guaranteed money, coming month after month, might change the way people behave. The idea that easy money makes people lazy, or worse, makes them dissolute (because they now have the time and money to smoke and drink), has a long pedigree in conservative economics and politics.

But there is also the more optimistic view, especially in recent years, that the money might actually grease the way towards making more, so that one rupee of UBI turns into several rupees of extra money for a household. Imagine someone – maybe a bit like how I was once upon a time – whose dream is to quit her job as a cook in a household and run a small restaurant. Maybe just a stall by the roadside in Kolkata, with a couple of makeshift benches and a tarp overhead, where she can serve her favourite *dimer dalna* (eggs cooked in a cumin-accented sauce with potatoes) and *kumror chokka* (collapsed pumpkin in a gingery fry with black chickpeas and some rice) for people who need to take a break from their busy days. What stops her, maybe, is the fact she can't afford the *tola* that the local dadas imperiously (and illegally) demand from anyone who wants to occupy a piece of the sidewalk. Now, thanks to UBI, she can scrounge together just about enough. Or maybe she does have the cash, but what is holding her back is the fear that no one would like her cooking (she knows she is a good cook, but people are strange) and she would lose it all. And perhaps the fact that she has UBI to fall back on helps. Or it could be something more psychological: life has been too hard so far – her husband left and her son overdosed – and she just doesn't have the mental energy to take on anything new. The new money from UBI gives her a second wind and possibly with that comes a willingness to take a flyer.

Where Kenya slides into Lake Victoria, in its very west are some of that country's poorest counties. Eighty-five per cent of the population in Siaya and Bomet counties had experienced hunger in the one year before we surveyed them, following which Give Directly – a California-based NGO that believes in helping people by giving them cash – funded a UBI that covered *every* adult in forty-four villages. They were also guaranteed the local currency equivalent to 75 cents a day for twelve years.

Since there was much interest in the results from this intervention, the villages were chosen at random from a set of more than 300. A hundred other villages were chosen to be the control group, where no intervention was planned but similar data was collected. Another eighty got a short-term variant – the same monthly payments, but just for two years.

We now have some results from this study from exactly the point where the two-year intervention ended. And they do not disappoint.

For one, there is no evidence that getting UBI makes people lazy. They work more overall, not less, though the difference is small. They do cut back on working for others, but instead, are working more on their own projects. The number of non-farming businesses (shops and eating places, for instance) associated with these villages is almost a third higher than the villages where no intervention has happened. The number of farming businesses (like poultry and goat-herding) has gone up too. As a result, earnings are about 20 per cent higher than those in the control villages. They also eat better, are less depressed and are more likely to say that they happy.

The contrast with the impact of the two-year UBI is also instructive. Strikingly, even though they got the same amount of money over two years, those in the two-year villages started fewer new businesses. Instead, they acted as if they were very aware that the money would run out soon and that they needed to find ways to save as much of it as possible. New businesses are risky and require ongoing investments, and hence, these villagers invested their money, instead, in things that they were confident of holding onto – improving their existing farms, buying durables for the home and feeding their children better. The fact that the twelve-year UBI money was there for the foreseeable future seemed to encourage the other set of villagers to be a lot more adventurous.

As an economist, my first instinct is to resist the question of whether they are wasting the money, say, on drinks or cigarettes. After all, I am answerable to no one when I buy myself a bottle of wine. Indeed, it might even be seen as cool – as evidence that I know the good life. So, why should poor people be asked that question? But the world wanted that answer (and I guess, with anything addictive, there are real risks as well), so we collected data on various measures of alcohol consumption. The evidence, at one level, was clear:

the fraction of villagers who said they drank every day went down – and significantly so – with the twelve-year UBI. The question was whether they were just saying it to make us happy. To get around that, we also asked if others in the village were drinking too much and creating an issue for them, so that the responders had the option of staying 'pure'. Again, what we saw in the data was good news – problem drinking had gone down. On the other hand, sales at the local liquor stores had gone up. I hope that is because people are buying fancier forms of alcohol instead of getting drunk on home brew.

New year's days are always a little complicated because they offer us the option (and the pressure) of a new start (and a reminder of all those old starts that went nowhere). A nice meal never hurts, and here is one that draws on North-African, Japanese and French cooking.

CUCUMBER COCKTAIL

1 KG LARGE CUCUMBERS

½ CUP ELDERFLOWER LIQUOR/SWEET VERMOUTH

1 CUP VODKA

2 TBSP LIME JUICE

2 TBSP STEVIA POWDER (OPTIONAL)

ICE CUBES

FOR GARNISH

5–6 MINT LEAVES

▶ Make 1 cup of clear cucumber juice by putting in 1 kg (peeled and chopped) cucumbers into a blender and straining the resulting liquid through a cheesecloth. Put the juice into a cocktail shaker along with 1 cup vodka, ½ cup elderflower liquor (or sweet vermouth) and 2 tbsp lime juice. Shake well. This concoction is sweet enough, but if you prefer your mocktails sweeter, add 2 tbsp stevia syrup to this. To make the stevia syrup, heat 1 cup of water with 2 tbsp stevia powder, and once it is fully dissolved, let it cool.

Pour the above concoction over ice in a cocktail glass and garnish with slightly bruised mint leaves.

MOROCCAN-INSPIRED LAMB ROAST

1½ KG LAMB SHOULDER

¼ CUP OLIVE OIL

4 TBSP CHOPPED CILANTRO

3 TBSP BUTTER

3 TBSP LEMON JUICE

2 TSP FLOUR

2 TSP SALT

1½ TSP CORIANDER POWDER

1 TSP GINGER POWDER

1 TSP CUMIN POWDER

1 TSP TURMERIC POWDER

¾ TSP QUATRE ÉPICES/GARAM MASALA

3 GARLIC CLOVES

3 DRY ROSEBUDS (OPTIONAL)

A PINCH OF CAYENNE

▶ Make deep gashes on the lamb on both sides. Blend ¼ cup olive oil, 4 tbsp chopped cilantro, 3 tbsp lemon juice, 2 tsp salt, 1½ tsp coriander powder, 1 tsp each of ginger powder, turmeric powder, cumin powder, ¾ tsp garam masala, 3 garlic cloves, 3 rosebuds and a pinch of cayenne. Rub this spice paste all over the lamb, coating it nicely on all sides. Cover the lamb tightly in an aluminium foil and place it in a baking dish. Bake for 3 hours at 160°C.

When the lamb is done, keep it covered for 10 more minutes, then take out the accumulated juices. In a small saucepan, melt 2 tbsp butter, whisk in 2 tsp of flour and add the juices from the lamb. Cook till the sauce thickens and finish by adding 1 tbsp of melted butter.

ALMOND–STONE FRUIT UPSIDE-DOWN CAKE

750 GM STONE FRUIT (PLUMS, PEACHES, NECTARINES)

225 GM ALMOND FLOUR

150 GM MELTED BUTTER

3 LARGE EGGS

¾ CUP SUGAR (OR 3 TBSP STEVIA POWDER)

½ CUP SOUR CREAM

⅓ CUP HONEY

1 TBSP SUGAR

1 TSP BAKING POWDER

 ▶ Line a 9" cakepan with parchment paper buttered so that it does not stick to the bottom of the pan. Cover the cakepan with slices of stone fruits (with the stones taken out). Sprinkle 1 tbsp sugar over them.

In a food processor, add ⅓ cup honey, 3 large eggs, ½ cup sour cream and 150 gm melted butter. Beat well, making sure the honey gets integrated well into the mixture. Add 225 gm almond flour, ¾ cup sugar or 3 tbsp stevia, 1 (heaped) tsp baking powder and blend well. Bake at 180°C for 50 minutes, covering with foil for the last 10 minutes if it is browning too fast. Turn the cake over onto a platter, flipping it in the process so that the fruits come out on top.

India's Protein Problem

My grandfather had his ways of being annoying – such as spending a lot of money that he did not have – but his social sympathies were broad. His best friend, for many years, was a Muslim – they went together to Edinburgh to study back in 1938 – and I cannot recall him expressing any serious prejudices. But when it came to cricket, his theory of why we Indians didn't have any good fast bowlers (this was the 1970s) came down to: '*Ora to shader dalna khay*'. (They, Muslims from Pakistan, our regular tormentors, eat curried bulls [and we don't].)

I didn't have access to Wikipedia back then and perhaps had no reason to question his wisdom. It turns out that per capita annual meat consumption is very similar in India and Bangladesh, and very little (4 kilograms a year). It is much higher in Pakistan (16 kilograms), but the corresponding number for China is four times as much and that for the US is eight times bigger. Meat is simply not an important part of the South Asian nutritional profile, even though it has an important social role to play. Celebration for Christians and Muslims but also Bengali Hindus has a special place for meat dishes. In my grandfather's ancestral village, now a part of Kolkata, water buffaloes were sacrificed during Kali puja to affirm our *shakta* credentials. My grandfather offered to take me when I was seven or so. I demurred, petrified by just the idea.

This was before the time of Javagal Srinath, the famously vegetarian fast bowler; much before the time of the unabashedly macho Hardik Pandya, who brings a cook with him when he travels to support his vegetarian diet, or the brilliant Ravi Ashwin, who isn't a fast bowler but definitely has the height and the muscles to be one. Even the gentle Jaspreet Bumrah, who so terrifies batsmen around the world with his fast bowling, talks about his fealty to traditional, mostly vegetarian, Punjabi food. Being vegetarian is no barrier to being big and strong.

Why then, if it is not due to our primarily (but for the most part, not exclusively) vegetarian diet, is India the stunting and wasting capital of the world? According to WHO, we have the second-highest fraction of children under five who are radically underweight for their heights (in other words, wasted). And before blaming poverty, note that this puts us below civil-war-torn Yemen, Eritrea, Somalia and Sudan, and at least fifty other countries – mostly in Africa and Asia – that are all poorer than us (in many cases, much poorer). The Democratic Republic of Congo (DRC), for example, has a per capita GDP – adjusted for purchasing power – that is one-eighth of ours, but their wasting rates are less than half as much.

Inequality matters, of course – a lot of that per capita income goes to the rich. But even if we compare poverty rates, DRC, by the World Bank metric, has almost thrice as many poor people as us. Even within India, richer states like Gujarat and Maharashtra, with relatively low poverty rates, have among the highest wasting (and stunting, i.e., low height for age) rates.

It is not genetics either. Indian children born and brought up in the UK are no more wasted or stunted at five than the local population, even though their immigrant parents are shorter. And perhaps, more tellingly, as the insightful research by my friends Seema Jayachandran (from Princeton) and Rohini Pande (from Yale) shows,[14] while the average Indian child is shorter than the average child in the much poorer countries in sub-Saharan Africa, the oldest male child in Indian families is actually taller. This is not the case for the oldest female child or the other family members, male or female.

The same facts also tell us that while unsanitary conditions, unclean water and the resulting prevalence of diarrhoeal diseases is an important reason why Indians grow up short, it cannot be the whole story since (a) open defecation is an even bigger problem in many African countries and (b) firstborn boys and other children from the same families presumably grow up under the same environmental conditions.

Jayachandran and Pande argue that a lot of the problem comes down to the resolute preference for the oldest male child among Hindu families (the gap between the first-born boy and the rest is substantially smaller among Indian Muslims). We apparently lavish all our resources and attention on that lucky boy, letting the others fend for themselves. He does benefit, but what the rest lose is tragically larger (which makes me, as the oldest male child and the tallest in my family, start to feel slightly embarrassed).

Jayachandran and Pande's assessment is that this misallocation of resources within the family can, by itself, explain perhaps half of the India–Africa gap. For the rest of the gap, it is true that the share of food in total spending is lower in India than in most comparable countries – including Pakistan and Bangladesh (both of which do much better in terms of child wasting despite being poorer) – but it is not clear how much of that is because grains are heavily subsidized under the Food Security Act.

Indeed, the problem in India might be precisely that we get too many of our calories from grains and too little from proteins. The recent EAT–Lancet reference diet[15] suggests that people should get 29 per cent of their calories from proteins. While there is probably a margin of error, the recent estimate[16] by a team led by Manika Sharma at International Food Policy Research Institute (IFPRI) in Delhi suggests that rural Indians get just 6 per cent of their calories from proteins, which is quite worrying. Even the richest Indians in the National Sample Survey (NSS) data get only about half of the recommended amount. The problem, to come back to where we started, is not the absence of meat – the EAT–Lancet-recommended diet is mostly vegetarian – but the absence of other, more sustainable proteins.

In West Africa, peanuts are that source of protein. In much of India, peanuts are what we eat while waiting for better things. Changing dietary attitudes is not easy – especially for those who are not addicted to MasterChef Australia – but perhaps public feeding programmes (say during social or religious celebrations) offer an opportunity. My taste for the wonderful, thick Punjabi dals, to take an example, came out of visits to a langarkhana at a nearby gurdwara. I can still picture myself, seventeen and gawky, hesitating by the door in the winter sun, guilty for eating free what I could afford to buy. Then, distracted by the wafting fragrances and my rising greed, I stepped right in.

Maafe is from West Africa while socca is from the south of France, as is the inspiration behind the paneer-stuffed tomatoes (though the local goat's cheese would be used instead of paneer). They are all meant to be inexpensive ways to feed the family and get some protein.

MAAFE

500 GM SWEET POTATO

500 GM PUMPKIN

400 GM CHICKEN (LEGS AND THIGHS)

1 LITRE VEGETABLE/CHICKEN STOCK

4 CUPS SPINACH (OR MOOLI/SHALGUM GREENS)

⅔ CUP CHOPPED ONION

2 PLANTAINS

2 CARROTS

3 CLOVES GARLIC

4 TBSP DOUBLE-CONCENTRATED TOMATO PASTE

4–6 TBSP OIL (ANY NEUTRAL OIL)

3 TBSP UNSWEETENED PEANUT BUTTER

1 TBSP GRATED GINGER

1 SLICED RED CHILLI

1 TSP TURMERIC POWDER

1 TSP SALT

½ TSP BLACK PEPPER

¼ TSP CHILLI POWDER

 ▶ Peel 500 gm sweet potato, 500 gm pumpkin, 2 plantains and 2 carrots, and chop them into 1" pieces. Add 400 gm (ideally) organic, bone-in, free-range chicken meat – cut into 1½" pieces – from the legs and thighs. In a large, heavy saucepan, heat 4 tbsp of any neutral oil at medium low heat and throw in the chopped vegetables. When they start getting a reddish tint, add the chicken pieces and brown quickly (for about 2 minutes). Remove from heat, and separate the plantain chunks and chicken pieces.

Put the saucepan back at medium heat, adding oil (if necessary) so that at least 2 tbsp oil is present in the saucepan. Once the oil is hot, add ⅔ cup chopped onion along with 3 cloves of coarsely chopped garlic. Cook for about 5 minutes till the onions start turning brown. Turn the heat to low and add 1 tbsp grated ginger, 1 sliced red chilli and 4 tbsp double-concentrated tomato paste. Gently stir them into the oil.

Add 1 litre of vegetable/chicken stock, 1 tsp turmeric powder, ¼ tsp chilli powder, 1 tsp of salt and few turns of a pepper grinder, and bring to boil. Add the plantains, set the heat to medium low and cook for 10 minutes. Put in the rest of the vegetables (not the chicken). Cover and cook for 20 minutes at medium low.

Remove ¼ cup of the vegetable-infused broth and mix 3 tbsp unsweetened peanut butter in it. Add it back into the cooking broth, turn the heat to low, and add 4 cups of washed spinach (or mooli/shalgum greens) with the thick stalks removed. Also add the chicken. Cook for 15 minutes. Check for salt and spiciness as per taste.

SOCCA

1 CUP CHICKPEA FLOUR

2 TBSP OLIVE OIL

½ TSP SALT

1 TSP FENNEL SEEDS

 ▶ Mix 1 cup chickpea flour with 1 cup water, 1¼ tbsp of olive oil, 1 tsp fennel seeds and ½ tsp salt. Knead into a dough, cover with a kitchen towel and set aside for 30 minutes.

Heat up a cast-iron pan for 5 minutes on high heat. Very carefully, take the pan off the heat and place it on a safe surface. Cover the surface with ½ tbsp of olive oil. Flatten the dough onto the hot pan using a spatula (very carefully). Put the batter into the oven and place under the preheated broiler for 7 minutes at 250°C. Do not flip it. It should turn brown at the edges, coming off the surface. Take it off using a metal spatula.

Serve the socca with a nutritious chutney or as a roti with dal and achaar, or like the French, with a tomato salad or a wonderful olive paste called tapenade (which is also super nutritious).

PANEER-STUFFED TOMATOES

4 LARGE BEEFSTEAK (OR OTHER ROUND) TOMATOES

1 CUP COOKED CHICKPEAS

½ CUP PANEER OR OTHER RELATIVELY BLAND CHEESE

½ CUP ZUCCHINI

6 OLIVES

5 FIGS

1 TBSP LEMON JUICE

1 TSP OLIVE OIL

1 TSP PAPRIKA

SALT (TO TASTE)

 ▶ Cut the tomatoes horizontally at the top, removing the part where the stem connects to it. Using a spoon, scoop out the flesh and discard; be mindful not to pierce the skin. Keep the top to use as a cover later.

Preheat the oven to 200°C.

Grate the zucchini and add salt to it. Press the grated shreds to get rid of the excess water. Add 1 cup of mashed chickpeas, 6 pitted and chopped olives, 5 chopped figs, 1 tbsp lemon juice, 1 tsp olive oil, 1 tsp paprika and salt (to taste) to the shreds.

Stuff the tomatoes with the zucchini mixture, cover them with the tops, drizzle a tiny bit of olive oil over each tomato and bake for 20 minutes in a baking pan. When done, the skin should be wrinkled.

Adapting to Hot Summers

As a child, I remember quite liking the searing heat of the high summer, that sense of being almost erased by the sun's fierce gaze. There was high drama to be enjoyed: the sudden, fierce gusts, the quick-darkening clouds called forth, I used to think, by the earth's thirsty protests, the fleeting rain that dries almost as soon as it hits the ground, the bright light after it all passes, the grateful scent of the quenched earth . . . all of that I used to love. One of my most vivid memories from when I was six is being caught in one of these summer storms, running home through an orchard of pomelo trees, dodging the heavy pomelos that the storm was scattering around the garden, and then running out, as soon as the storm subsided, to collect the pomelos and green mangoes that it left behind on the ground. It didn't hurt that early summer was the start of the mango season in Bengal, with the delicate heemsagars making their first appearances accompanied by the wonderful kanche meethe aam, the half-sweet green mangoes that go perfectly with a dressing of chilli, chaat masala and kashundi, Bengal's marvellous answer to French mustard.

All that deliciousness is thankfully still there. It is the weather that is turning on us. As I write, daytime temperatures in large parts of India are hitting a potentially lethal 45 degrees Celsius. We all know that this is not accidental and that what is coming is even worse. Just one more day in the year when the district average temperature goes above 35 degree Celsius (rather than staying in the more temperate 22–24 degree range) pushes the annual death rates in that district by 0.7 per cent, according to the careful work[17] done by my friends and colleagues, Robin Burgess, Dave Donaldson and Micheal Greenstone (along with Olivier Deschenes). This mostly happens in the countryside, where people need to work outside. Moreover, those very hot days are predicted to go from about five a year (presently) to seventy-five by the end of the century, if climate change is allowed to continue unabated (God forbid). In terms of brute numbers, it says that life expectancy will be 10.5 years less for rural Indians born between 2075 and 2099, compared to those born in 2000.

While recognizing just how frightening this is, and the need for urgent and decisive action, it is easy to lose track of the fact that most of us (hopefully) will need to go on living, and ideally, enjoying it. The current discourse on climate change is so dire that pleasure has no place in it, but it is hard to win a fight as big as one against global warming without reminding people of *what* they are fighting for.

Our reaction to the doomsday discourse right now is almost purely defensive: people are buying air conditioners in record numbers. There are estimates that the number of households in India with air conditioning will go up fifteen-fold by 2050. This would be a very different India: an enormous part of today's socialization for everyone except the elites happens in the streets and the neighbourhoods, in college courtyards and roadside dhabas, through tennis-ball cricket and pavement badminton. If people stop going out for a big part of the year because it is too hot and wrap themselves in their air-conditioned cocoons, if mothers stop children from going out to play, if friends no longer congregate in ramshackle tea shops or under some shady tree (as we used to), if relatives don't not walk over for random visits, the society will be unrecognizably altered without anyone trying to change it.

Of course, there are other reasons to worry about this explosion in air conditioners. It is estimated that we will need a thousand 600-megawatt (read huge) power plants just to run the air conditioners. This, by itself, will push India into the highest global ranks for carbon guzzling, unleashing a murderous cycle where our own demand for comfort will drive further increases in temperatures and make life even more impossible for those who cannot afford the protection of technology.

A big part of the problem is that the air conditioners we presently use in India are often extremely wasteful of energy.

They are also very cheap. One of the open secrets of marketing is that low upfront costs and high usage charges make sales easier (think of the attractively priced printers that then fleece you on the price of ink). To make matters worse, many of the new buyers lack the ready cash to buy high-quality machines, though they might know that they would eventually regret not buying them. We need to act fast on this, making it impossible to buy the carbon gluttons while offering easy loans and discounts to make the efficient ones affordable. This can apparently cut power consumption by a factor of five.

But these technologies won't solve the problem of growing isolation. For that, we will need to reimagine our public spaces. Ultra-hot days are nothing new in India. One simple rule that we all used to survive high-school history exams was that good kings planted trees, dug wells and built saraikhanas where sun-weary travellers could refresh themselves (bad kings destroyed places of worship). Most governments in India pay lip service to planting trees – much of urban India is shockingly bare. Growing the right kind of trees takes time, but it is one of the best-known antidotes to hot weather. In the meanwhile, my hope/fantasy is that there will be shelters along the roads and in parks and playgrounds – with water to drink and some kind of cooling technology – open to everyone during the hot hours to break away from the heat and refresh themselves. Inside these shelters could be stalls selling something cheap and delicious like tart and spicy nimbu pani with a dash of kala namak, sattu ka sharbat (shaved ice with a brightly coloured shot of fruit flavouring), mango-flavoured iced tea or just cold water with slices of cucumbers steeping in it. What is important is that it remains a democratic space – a cooler (in all senses of the word) version of the tea shops we used to frequent, where one could spend hours for the price of a cup and even the local rickshaw puller did not feel uncomfortable stepping in for a quick drink.

Some of this, especially the construction of shelters, will surely need state intervention and support. But to make anything function well at the Indian scale, with all its million local variations, communities need to act. In Gujarat and Rajasthan, villages used to have their own summer defence – stepwells. These were gigantic underground living spaces built around a well, cooled by the evaporation of the well water during the blazing summer months. I suspect there were many things about them that I would not have liked – the segregation of women, the exclusion of those from the lower castes, for instance – but I am also sure they did much to give summer its own respite and delight. In my imagination, the guests were served plates of chilled and salted jamun, along with perhaps my most favourite fruit drink – a sharbat made from falsa. We need some of that joy too, if we want to avoid falling into the gulag of air-conditioned isolation, whether it is sitting in the shade of a beautiful tree (especially if there is a small, cooling breeze), reading something or just ruminating, or drinking something cold – lightly sweet or slightly savoury – with friends, ideally with a prospect of a mango later when it gets a bit cooler.

Here are a few of my summer favourites from all over the world. They have the advantage of being very simple to prepare (you don't want to have to work hard when the weather demands cooling down) and refreshing in different ways.

MEXICAN(ISH) HORCHATA

1 CUP RAW RICE

1½ CUPS COLD MILK

⅓ CUP SUGAR (OR SWEETENER)

½ CUP BLANCHED ALMONDS (SLICED)

1 TSP ROSE/VANILLA ESSENCE

1" STICK CINNAMON

▶ In a blender, add 1 cup raw rice (preferably any fragrant variety), ½ cup blanched almonds (sliced), 1" stick of cinnamon and 3 cups of cold water. Blend for 3–4 minutes, stopping the blender a few times (if required) to prevent overheating. Chill this mixture overnight and then strain, first through a tea strainer and then through a muslin cloth. Repeat the process (if needed) to remove all the grit.

To the rice mixture, add 3 cups of cold water, 1½ cups of cold milk, ⅓ cup sugar (or sweetener) and 1 tsp rose or vanilla essence (or both). Mix well till the sugar dissolves in the liquid.

VIETNAMESE-INSPIRED MANGO TEA

1 CUP RIPE MANGO FLESH

2 TBSP SUGAR (OR SWEETENER)

2 REGULAR TEA BAGS

A PINCH OF BLACK PEPPER

 ▶ Peel and thinly slice one (or more) ripe, sweet mango(es) to get 1 cup of mango flesh. Place the flesh in a small saucepan with 2 tbsp sugar (or sweetener) and cook at low heat for 7–8 minutes till the mango softens and releases its juices. Remove from heat and let it cool.

While the mango flesh is cooking, boil 2 cups of water and add 2 regular tea bags into it, soaking them for 5 minutes. Add this to the mango mixture with a pinch of black pepper. Then add two cups of cold water and chill for 2 hours. You can make this Vietnamese-inspired tea using peaches and nectarines as well.

MOROCCAN-STYLE CUCUMBER WATER

150 GM CUCUMBER
8 CUPS COLD WATER

 ▶ Fill a jug with 8 cups of cold water and add 150 gm thinly sliced cucumber into it. Chill in the fridge for a few hours and your refreshing drink is ready.

Unfair
Imprisonments

n May 1983, I was one of the 350-odd JNU students who ended up in Tihar Jail. I don't recall what it was about, but it led to the president of the student union being expelled, which we felt was an egregious assault on our democratic rights. The vice chancellor's house was occupied. The police showed up in full riot gear, with clear instructions to make it an example. Some got arrested on the spot; others courted arrest in solidarity.

I thought then – and I still believe – that the authorities deliberately provoked the fight so that they could show us who the boss was. Many of the famously 'liberal' rules at JNU, such as the ability to have female guests in your room during the day hours, got rescinded after the bust-up even though nobody explained what that had to do with the protests.

Tihar Jail was famous. We had read all about Charles Sobhraj, the 'bikini killer', who was imprisoned there at the time. He would famously escape from there in 1986, but this was after a good bunch of our group of JNU students – men and women – had already done it.

I didn't escape, but mostly because it seemed slightly undignified; the technology was easy enough. Unlike Charles Sobhraj, we were not seen as escape risks and hence, the police were not paying attention.

As I remember it, albeit through the rose-tinted lens of nostalgia, I quite enjoyed the days in Tihar. It was May in Delhi. Very hot. No fans. And very little to do. Some visitors brought us a pack of cards. One could play volleyball, but I was so bad at it that I risked breaking my fingers. Eventually, there were a few books to share. And there was the novelty of the situation, the enforced rest, and being with so many of my friends.

I had worried that food would be a problem. Indeed, my one immediate regret was that I missed my first meal at Bukhara, home of the eponymous dal. My aunt was going to take me there, I think, the very evening I ended up in Tihar. The first day, we got roti and dal. Two times a day. That's it (as far as I can remember). Some of our savvier classmates figured out that this was in breach of the rules. In the bizarre hierarchy of the Indian Penal Code (IPC), we, as postgraduate students, had a right to a vegetable on top of our dal and roti. We complained. The prison authorities pushed back: not all of us were postgraduates – there was a small number of students from the School of Languages, who were only one or two years into their five-year integrated master's program. Hence, not eligible. One of our colleagues, later a prominent member of the civil services, threatened a fast (until death or liberation?).

I must say, I cringed – there we were, mostly left-wing activists, demanding special favours based on our privileged education that less educated prisoners would never get. But that threat carried the day and I was happy to eat the vegetables. This being summer, it was often bhindi. I didn't complain. I must have been four, and in the US, when I discovered the pleasure of bhindi – dry fried with onions – and roti. It remains one of my favourite things to eat.

The British left us with the idea that the socially privileged should be treated better even in prison. Blinded by caste and other distinctions, we did not bother to change this even after they left. Indeed, remarkably until the introduction of the Model Prisons Act in May 2023, prisons in India were governed by the Prisons Act of 1894 from a time when our rulers were happy to put up signs saying: 'Dogs and Indians not allowed'. And while I suspect change is coming, till as late as January 2024 – months after the Model Act – the Supreme Court was berating the states for caste discrimination in prisons. Apparently, Brahmins get to work in the prison kitchens while the lowest castes are assigned toilet duties.

Perhaps an even bigger problem is that of undertrials. A remarkable 77 per cent of those imprisoned in India have not been convicted; they are waiting to be tried. More than a quarter of those have been in jail for a year or more, nearly 3 per cent for *more than five years.* A significant number have been under trial for as many as ten years and at least for some of them, the maximum sentence for the crime they are accused of is less than ten years.

This is not a new problem. In 1979, a Law Commission complained about it. The ratio of undertrials among the imprisoned was then 58 per cent (now it's nearly 80 per cent). The source of the problem is an incredible logjam in the Indian court system. There are 50 million cases pending in Indian courts, including 170,000 that have been in court for 30 years or more! That number was still an impressive 29 million in 2018, when the government's think tank Niti Aayog concluded that at the current rate, it would take 324 years to dispose of all the pending cases. And while we are a litigious people, this is also because we have 21 sanctioned judgeships per million population (while the US has 150) and only two-thirds of these are currently filled.

One consequence of a broken system is that it hurts those who are least able to work around its deficiencies. In India, half the undertrials are from socially marginal groups – SCs, STs and Muslims – that constitute only about a third of the population. Overrepresentation of socially weaker groups in prisons, unfortunately, is common enough across the world. In the US, African Americans constitute just 13 per cent of the total population but 40 per cent of the imprisoned. A lot of this is pure discrimination, but in India, it is also the way the system works. Thinking back to our time in Tihar, what shocks me now is just how unbothered we were. We assumed that, eventually, the very serious charges levelled at us (attempt to murder was, impressively, one of them) would get dropped. Our presumption was based less on our (true) innocence than on the idea that the collective parents of this group were too powerful to let anything happen to their brood.

Consider, by comparison, a boy who just happened to be hanging out with a group that got rounded up after a spot of trouble. He is fifteen and should be treated as a juvenile, but has no way to prove it. He can barely read. Illiterates are 50 per cent more likely to be in prison compared to their share in the population of younger males who constitute, like everywhere else, most of the imprisoned. He does not understand bail and his mother cannot afford a lawyer. The state-provided lawyer is young, inexperienced and used to getting bullied by the police. The judge is too busy and too harassed to do anything about it. There are other more important cases in his court and he gets many calls from powerful people. But he worries that the police want to keep the boy – not because they have anything on him, but because they want to look like they have some leads and know he is powerless. The judge knows that they can even hold him after bail gets granted because there is often no follow up. The boy knows nothing of all that. He is a little frightened but doesn't know what he should worry about. Sometimes, he prays like his mother has told him to, but mostly, he daydreams and waits for mealtimes. He would not say this to his mum, but he prefers the way they make bhindi in Tihar.

These very simple desi vegetable dishes are, for me, some of the glories of world cuisine – as good as any way to treat vegetables that I have eaten elsewhere in the world.

MY MOTHER'S BHINDI FRY

750 GM BHINDI (LADY FINGER)

1 TSP TURMERIC POWDER

1 TSP SALT

400 GM ONIONS

5 TBSP RAPESEED/SUNFLOWER OIL

1 TSP PANCHPORAN

1–2 DRIED RED CHILLI(S)

▶ Take 750 gm bhindi, and cut the tops and the tips off. Then cut the bhindi horizontally into slices the thickness of your pinkie finger (4-mm approx). Marinate the slices in 1 tsp turmeric powder and 1 tsp salt for 30 minutes.

In the meantime, dice 400 gm onions into bits, roughly comparable to the bhindi slices. In a large frying pan (11" or more), heat 5 tbsp of rapeseed/sunflower oil at medium high, and toss in 1 tsp panchporan and 1–2 dried red chilli(es). When the seeds stop popping, add the bhindi and the onions, and coat the vegetables in the hot oil. Reduce the heat to medium and fry for 20 minutes or so, until the vegetables start turning a nice, winey red.

TART AND NUTTY BHINDI

500 GM BHINDI (LADY FINGER)

2 RED CHILLIES

3 TBSP RAPESEED/SUNFLOWER OIL

1 TBSP CHANA DAL

1 TSP TURMERIC POWDER

1 TSP SALT

1 TSP BROWN MUSTARD SEEDS

1 TSP AAMCHUR POWDER

A SPRIG OF CURRY LEAVES

A PINCH OF HING

▶Take 500 gm small bhindi, and cut the tops and tips off. Then cut the bhindi in half from top to bottom. Put the halves into a colander, marinate in 1 tsp turmeric powder and 1 tsp salt, and set aside for 30 minutes.

In a large frying pan (11" or more), heat 3 tbsp rapeseed/sunflower oil at medium high and throw in 1 tsp brown mustard seeds. When the popping starts to slow down, add 2 red chillies, 1 tbsp chana dal, a sprig of curry leaves and a pinch of hing. After 1 minute, add the bhindi, face down. Reduce the heat to medium and let it cook for 8 minutes. Turn it over, cook for 5 more minutes or till the skin side starts to turn brown. Remove from heat and set the bhindi out on some paper towels. Dust with 1 tsp of aamchur powder.

AKEELA'S KARELA

2 KARELAS (BITTER GOURDS)

3 TBSP OIL

3 TBSP CILANTRO

3 TBSP FRIED CASHEW NUTS

2 TSP JAGGERY OR BROWN SUGAR

1 TSP AAMCHUR POWDER

1 TSP TURMERIC POWDER

½ TSP CUMIN SEEDS

½ TSP MUSTARD SEEDS

½ TSP CUMIN POWDER

½ TSP CORIANDER POWDER

¼ TSP CAYENNE POWDER

SALT (TO TASTE)

A PINCH OF HING

A SPRIG OF CURRY LEAVES

▶ Slice two karelas into super thin slices, and marinate in 1 tsp salt and 1 tsp turmeric powder for 30 minutes. Steam the slices for about 5 minutes and discard the water. In a frying pan, heat 3 tbsp oil, and fry ½ tsp cumin seeds and ½ tsp mustard seeds. Then, add a good pinch of hing. Toss in the steamed karela slices along with a sprig of curry leaves and fry at low heat after adding ½ tsp cumin powder, ½ tsp coriander powder, ¼ tsp cayenne powder, 1 tsp aamchur powder, 2 tsp jaggery (or brown sugar) and salt (to taste). Once the spices are nicely incorporated, remove from heat and add 3 tbsp chopped cilantro and 3 tbsp fried cashew nuts.

Conspicuous
Consumption

After a week of virtual immersion in the Ambani festivities, an indignant friend asked me: 'This Ambani wedding, why would anyone do something like that?', 'Such extravagance – won't people in your country get upset? Won't the Ambanis get into trouble?'

I said no.

Why was I so sure? It was extravagant – the most expensive wedding anywhere on the globe in modern memory. Estimates of the amount spent seem to be in the range of 500 million US dollars, including the groom's multimillion dollar watch and several million more in watches for the twenty-five best men (all best?) at a quarter million dollars a pop.

And the food. One Instagrammer claims that 2,500-odd dishes were served over the days of the celebration, all vegetarian. My attempt to list all the vegetarian dishes I know finished well below a thousand, so perhaps this is an exaggeration, but clearly many hundreds were served. It made me think what I would do faced with so much choice: there is a justly famous experiment by Sheena Iyengar and Mark Lepper[18] showing that when buyers in a supermarket were offered twenty-four different jams and preserves to choose from, rather than just six, they were actually less likely to go home with a jam. The plethora of choices ends up paralysing the chooser. I suspect something like that would happen to me at the chaat stand at the Ambani wedding that was much written about, though the tamatar ki chaat I surely would not have missed.

So, it was an exercise in excess and a very visible one. Why wasn't it seen as a potentially provocative act in a country where the total annual spending on MGNREGA, the Indian government's most important anti-poverty programme covering nearly 15 crore beneficiaries, is only about ten times the amount spent on this wedding? Why would 15,000 people get to enjoy over a few days, what could be an economic lifeline for 1.5 crore people for an entire year?

Did the Ambanis expect it to be unpopular but assume that their power will protect them? I don't think so. Mr Narendra Modi and Ms Mamata Banerjee attended and they are both very savvy political spirits, representing very different constituencies and unlikely to touch anything that the public hates.

The most likely answer is that most Indians, unlike my (non-Indian) friend, didn't see this as something particularly offensive. After all, in late-nineteenth- and early-twentieth-century Bengal, neighbouring zamindars with too much money and too little to do literally organized weddings for their cats (*biraler biye*) and even their ponds (*pukurer biye*) just so that they could enjoy a great party. This was at a time when many people lived on one meal a day in these zamindar's villages.

My guess is that the average low-income Indian expects very little of the very rich. Indeed, our wealthy have so often trampled on the rights of the rest – to take a particularly awful example, zamindars insisting that they get to deflower every new bride – that the poor might be grateful as long as they are left to their own devices. For many others, the point is simple: we have chosen an economic system (for better, or likely, for worse) that enables breathtaking wealth accumulation. Why then fret about the way the wealthy spend their wealth? Maybe better a spectacle like this one, where lots of jobs get created in feeding the guests and in making flower arrangements, than buying expensive paintings or funding classical music. And since everyone in India tries to do their best for their children's weddings, why not the Ambanis?

What it does mean, however, is that we shouldn't be swayed by the right-wing idea that taxes on the rich need to be low because they are uniquely positioned to create jobs and incomes by investing their wealth. Buying expensive watches made in Europe does not count as investment.

The more interesting question to me is why all of this was worth it for the Ambanis. The great American social theorist, Thorstein Veblen, in his analysis of the rising American plutocracy of the late-nineteenth century[19], emphasized their need for legitimation. They consumed to show that they had arrived, to stake their claim for social influence against that of the previous generation of the rich – the Boston Brahmins, the New York 'aristocracy' (often of Dutch descent), the descendants of the Virginia tobacco growers and so on. And for that reason, their mansions needed to be bigger, their yachts much more lavish. Consumption, as Veblen noted, needed to be conspicuous.

But despite the obvious garishness, I don't think this explains the Ambani wedding. I don't think anyone in India needs to be persuaded that the Ambanis have arrived. Reliance is in every household, often in more forms than one. And while they are still not quite on the global firmament of the ultra-rich, they are savvy enough to know that some of their guests – Mark Zuckerberg (and several others), for instance – could have easily outspent them but opted not to. Moreover, as Veblen astutely pointed out, the compulsion to distinguish yourselves quite naturally seeks out originality and refinement:

> In order to avoid stultification, he must also cultivate his tastes, for it now becomes incumbent on him to discriminate with some nicety between the noble and the ignoble in consumable goods. He becomes a connoisseur in creditable viands of various degrees of merit, in manly beverages and trinkets, in seemly apparel and architecture, in weapons, games, dancers, and the narcotics.

In fact, gastronomy, as a category, is clearly associated with the rise of the bourgeoisie and its desire to challenge the aristocracy's hold on the high culture of France. It was not mere plenty that signalled the arrival of a new dominant class, but also the refinement of taste, exemplified by the very architectural cakes and pastries that Antonin Carême made famous in early-nineteenth-century Paris.

This is precisely what we did not see. There was good food, of course. Traditional Gujarati food was specifically mentioned, and I wished I had some details because my knowledge of that particular cuisine hardly extends beyond the wonderful khandvi and *oondhiyo*. Well-known restaurants across the world came with multiple cuisines. But the star turn, from what I read, might have come from the chaatwala. The emphasis was on comfort at a grand scale.

In the end, my theory of this particular wedding is perhaps uninteresting as a piece of social science. There was, if I had to guess, no ulterior motive behind the Ambani splurge – they did it because they could, because it was what they wanted. A party to end all parties, the last chance, perhaps, to have one in this generation with the full legitimacy that a wedding celebration affords. They did not want to be original, rather, just to affirm India's growing reputation as home to the most over-the-top wedding celebrations.

The fact that the Ambanis may not have been driven by social pressure does not mean that other Indians will not be. I worry that parents planning a wedding today might feel that they are not doing enough; of course, they can't match the Ambanis, but why not a bit more and just a bit more . . . Marianne Bertrand and Adair Morse from the University of Chicago have some interesting work[20] on what they call 'trickle-down consumption'. Apparently, in American states where the rich consume more in a particular year, the non-rich also end up consuming more in the same period, even when their incomes do not go up commensurately. They argue that this is either because the rich set the norms for consumption or the availability of more expensive consumer goods (more elaborate flower settings, fancier caterers, etc.) – because the rich want them – attracts the less affluent buyers, too. Either way, a lot of Indian parents already end up spending more on weddings than they can afford (especially since dowries, alas, have not gone away) and this particular show of wealth by the Ambanis probably hasn't helped.

Finally, all this makes me wish that our rich had different priorities, especially given that I don't see the political will to tax them much more. In a sense, the precise fact that the Ambanis were under no compulsion to spend the way they did suggests that if somebody in their family decides to go in a different direction, they would be free to do so. Some of the best-known foundations in the world – Rockefeller, Carnegie, Mellon, among others – came out of the Gilded Age, exactly the period and the culture that Veblen was writing about. In India, the Tatas and Azim Premji, among others, have already shown that there are other ways for the ultra-rich to spend their wealth, but it is clearly yet to take root. Maybe now that the weddings are over, the next extravagance can be an act of generosity that is even more visible than the Kardashians.

The urge to make something glorious and unexpected is something we all share. This is something easy enough to make, that has the right kind of oomph.

MANGO MOUSSE WITH NANKHATAI

FOR THE NANKHATAI

75 GM WHEAT FLOUR

65 GM SUGAR

60 GM GHEE

25 GM CHICKPEA FLOUR

¼ TSP BAKING POWDER

3 GREEN CARDAMOM PODS

FOR THE MOUSSE

250 GM MANGO PURÉE

250 GM FULL-FAT CREAM

40 GM SUGAR

3 GM GELATINE SHEETS

⅓ CUP PISTACHIOS

10 STRANDS OF SAFFRON

 ▶ To make the nankhatai, take a mixing bowl and mix together all the dry ingredients – wheat flour, sugar, chickpea flour and baking powder. Infuse the ghee with a cardamom pod. Grind the 2 remaining cardamom pods in the mixer and add to the dry mix.

Add the cardamom-infused ghee into the mixing bowl and lightly bring together the mixture with your fingers till it forms a dough that is crumbly but stiff. Divide the dough into 12 balls and slightly press them down. Bake for 10 minutes at 180°C.

To prepare the mango mousse, put the gelatine sheets in cold water to rehydrate. Add 250 gm full-fat cream with 40 gm sugar to a bowl and place the mixture in the fridge.

Meanwhile, gently heat 125 gm mango purée in a saucepan till it is just warm and throw in the saffron strands. Now, bring out the mixing bowl with the cream and sugar from the fridge, and whisk the mixture till the cream is close to being firm.

While the mango purée is still warm, melt in the gelatine and mix well. Add the other half of the mango purée, making sure that the mixture is lukewarm rather than cold (gently heat the spiced purée if need be). Add about one-third of the whipped cream and gently integrate into the purée. Now add the rest of the whipped cream using slow and regular movements till it is fully mixed.

Put the mousse in serving bowls and place these bowls in the fridge for 2 hours. Place a nankhatai on top and garnish the mousse with crushed, toasted pistachio bits before serving.

Thoughtful
Giving

I t was the first time I was invited to the kind of reception where important people go to meet even more important people. I was still young and *absolutely not important*, probably invited because the conference that led up to this reception needed populating. The food looked gorgeous. The jewelled red of the freshest tuna sashimi, golden spring rolls on a bed of diverse greens, small samosas next to a bright green sauce, tiny tarts with bright strawberries sitting regally on top, neat little sandwiches with the crusts cut off . . . and much more – a portfolio of the greatest hits of world canapé cuisine, echoing the other portfolios that were in discussion in this conclave of the global rich.

One theme that was making its hesitant way through that evening was the role of philanthropy. This was a long time ago, before the Gates Foundation became a global name. The role of philanthropists in the development process was only beginning to be discussed, but one could already hear the murmurs: 'governments are so corrupt, nothing really works', 'private schools work so much better'. My work on corruption was, in fact, the reason I was invited, but I suspect they had stopped reading before reaching my main point: if the private sector tried to do what the government does, they would face many of the same issues.

I was trying to animatedly explain that idea to a senior official from a development bank, and failing (I could tell by the way his eyes were drifting) when I noticed that trays of food had stopped coming. Since this was to be my dinner, it was my turn to be distracted. My explanations started to falter. It had just struck me that I had been fooled by the appearance of plenty – the food was there to signify munificence, not to fill us up.

Thinking back, it was, in a way, an appropriate metaphor for this world of high finance, where the flourish that goes into the discussion of 'giving back' sometimes dwarfs the actual amounts given. Of course, there are many who do take giving back very seriously and do it very well, and perhaps, even some who take it *too* seriously, as exemplified by the recent to-do about cryptocurrencies, Effective Altruism (EA) and FTX. Cryptocurrencies were born of the same suspicion of governments that I encountered during that evening, long before bitcoin was even a glint in the eye of its elusive creator. The idea was for the market to take over the government's role in supplying money. This, it was suggested, would work fine as long as no individual controlled more than a microscopic part of the money supply and the whole thing was coordinated by sophisticated cryptographic algorithms. It would also eliminate the risk of the government printing too many extra rupees to honour its commitments and thereby devaluing the currency. How well that has worked, I will leave you to judge: suffice to say that the value of the bitcoin, the oldest and most respected of these, has yo-yoed between 16,000 dollars and 60,000 dollars over the last two years. Think of the political backlash if this were the rupee or the dollar.

FTX was a crypto exchange where people could buy and sell the bewildering array of cryptocurrencies that are now available. Its founders were Effective Altruists, followers of a philosophy that takes the contempt for governments underlying the crypto project to its logical conclusion: if we cannot rely on the government to serve the poor and realize other societal goals, then socially minded private citizens should try to make as much money as they can and give it away. And if that requires bending some rules (or even just ignoring them), so be it, since it is in the ultimate social interest. And, as we know now, they did.

One can see how this same logic can encourage tax avoidance or even outright tax fraud. At a time when inequality is ballooning, this must worry governments that need to fund their many social commitments. According to the World Inequality Database, between 1995 and 2021, the wealth of the world's richest 750 people grew 2.5 times faster than the wealth of the top 1 per cent. Wealth is moving from the merely rich (the famous 1 per cent) to the super-duper rich, the kind of people who find it worthwhile to use tax havens and complicated strategies to dodge billions in taxes (think of Apple moving its intellectual property to Ireland to avoid paying the higher US taxes).

All of this might have been less worrying if this accumulating wealth was being used for the social good. Reliable numbers are scarce, but a valiant attempt by the Global Philanthropy Tracker (GPT) at the University of Indiana puts the total cross-border philanthropy in 2020 at 70 billion dollars. Not all of that money goes to the poor countries or is aimed at alleviating poverty. Quite a bit goes to the churches, mosques and temples, for one. Let us, in the absence of numbers, very optimistically assume that 35 billion dollars went to the world's poor. This is less than 2 dollars out of every extra 1,000 dollars that the world's richest 1 per cent accumulated *every year* between 2020 and 2023. Of course, there are other ways to serve the poorest – for example, investments that create jobs or inventions that slow global warming – but they still need education, healthcare and help when they cannot support themselves economically. The Government of India, alone, spends something like 220 billion dollars on that annually – seven times our estimate of global private generosity. Governments around the world fund a vast majority of the day-to-day fight against global poverty. Kind of like me filling up on a perfectly acceptable bowl of room-service pasta paid out of my own pocket, after missing out on the 'free' glam food at the reception.

Then there is the question of how the money gets spent. From my experience, the best philanthropic money is often extraordinarily useful precisely because it can identify important gaps – in programmes or in knowledge – and go a long way in filling them. But a lot of it echoes the style of that long-ago reception, a potpourri of the greatest hits. They change over time – perhaps, a burrata takes the place of spring rolls, and zaatar moves in for wasabi – but very slowly. I still attend receptions where I am told about the latest investment in microcredit and how it is transforming so many lives, and I hesitate to mention that it has been ten years since we – and then others – showed evidence that microcredit does not make the average beneficiary any richer.

The problem is that the rich are busy and the hyper-rich are hyper-busy. The attention it takes to do philanthropy well competes with many other concerns that are much more lucrative. Bill Gates' great insight was that he needed to do philanthropy full-time and really understand what works (and what doesn't), which explains why the Gates Foundation has been such a leader in the field. Too many others go for the easy option – some combination of what appeals to their gut instincts and what is in fashion, a bit like the canapés I did not get.

None of this is to say that there isn't an important place for philanthropy in the good fight. The best donors give much more than their money; they bring imagination, focus and an ability to think outside the box. They fund experiments, including ones inside governments, and have driven a significant part of improved delivery of public services. They highlight problems that deserve more attention and bring in expertise to solve them.

And in that spirit of more thoughtful giving, can I also hope for a more thoughtful reception menu? Maybe something that is less about glamour and fancy ingredients, and more about the harmony of tastes and colours. There is so much more to Chinese food, for example, than spring rolls, and to Indian food than samosas or chicken tangri kebabs, but I am yet to have been to a reception with either spiced jellyfish or kumror chokka. It is true that they are not natural finger foods, but there is a huge amount we can do with small tweaks on existing themes, like this recipe based on an eggplant bharta with South Indian spicing.

I added another wonderful example of a finger food that never makes it to the usual gatherings of 'influential people' – Balinese-style barbecued meat.

MILLEFEUILLE OF PAPAD AND BAIGAN BHARTA

750 GM BRINJAL(S)

200 GM TOMATOES

15 SMALL URAD DAL PAPADS

2 TBSP SUNFLOWER SEED OIL

2 TBSP TAHINI

1 SPRIG OF CURRY LEAVES

2 TSP URAD DAL

2 DRY RED CHILLIES

1 TSP BROWN MUSTARD SEEDS

1½ TSP SALT

A PINCH OF HING

▶ Place the brinjal(s) (750 gm) on an open fire, or in an oven at 200°C for 40 minutes, till fully soft. Peel the brinjal(s) and finely chop the flesh. In a frying pan, heat 2 tbsp sunflower seed oil and add 1 tsp brown mustard seeds to it. Once they stop popping, add a pinch of hing, 2 tsp urad dal, 2 dry red chillies and a sprig of curry leaves. Add the brinjal flesh along with 200 gm finely chopped tomatoes and 1½ tsp salt.

Add 2 tbsp tahini and let it cook for 20 minutes on low heat till it becomes a dryish paste. In the meantime, toast or lightly fry 15 small urad dal papads (more if you are using the tiny ones, which are better suited as finger food). Once the brinjal mixture has cooled, pick out the chillies and curry leaves from it. Make stacks of 5 papads and spoon in a layer of brinjal paste between each pair of papads to make your millefeuille.

BALINESE-STYLE BARBECUED MEAT

1 KG LAMB/PORK

½ CUP KECAP MANIS (INDONESIAN SWEET SOY SAUCE)

2 SHALLOTS

1 RED BELL PEPPER

1 FRESH RED CHILLI

1 STICK LEMON GRASS

3 LARGE CLOVES OF GARLIC

3 TBSP VEGETABLE OIL

1 TBSP CORIANDER POWDER

1 TSP TURMERIC POWDER

SALT (TO TASTE)

▶ Chop off the hard part of the lemon grass stick (on the top) and soak the lemon grass in hot water for 30 minutes. Then, in a blender, purée together ½ cup kecap manis (or regular dark soy with 3 tbsp brown sugar), 2 shallots, 1 red bell pepper, 1 fresh red chilli, 3 large cloves of garlic, 3 tbsp vegetable oil, 1 tbsp coriander powder, 1 tsp turmeric powder along with the previously soaked lemon grass and salt (keep in mind, the soy sauce is pretty salty, so adjust accordingly). The barbecue sauce is ready.

Take 1 kg lamb or pork (chopped into 1" cubes) and marinate the cubes in the barbecue sauce for 4 hours (or overnight). Put them on skewers and grill at medium high heat either on a barbecue, or in a pinch, under the grill of an oven. Check the internal temperature and remove when it reaches 65°C. Keep it covered for 10 minutes before serving.

Why I Won't Start a Restaurant

My wife and I are cowards: imaginary violence on a small computer screen scares us. We are, therefore, natural clients for the recent spate of TV and movie dramas about running restaurants, where a grease fire in the kitchen is mostly as stressful as it gets – the much-hyped (and rather silly) *The Menu* is a dramatic and highly missable exception. We loved *Boiling Point*, Philip Barantini's extraordinary single-take depiction of a busy night at a high-end restaurant. Cheyenne's sister Jade, a pastry chef who has worked at various high-end restaurants, tells us that the film captures well the feel of a restaurant kitchen when it's buzzing. She is also a fan of the TV serial *The Bear*, with Jeremy Allen-White (of underwear ad fame) as the chef and the main character.

The interest in restaurant stories is not accidental. We are in the age of the great chef, the stovetop sorcerer, the punctilious poet of the pasta pot. And it is entirely fair. Many chefs are extraordinarily creative, though I sometimes wish that Bandana (my late aunt) and Rama (who used to cook for my late mum) get even a fraction of their recognition. My aunt made the most divine *kochu bata* (spiced puréed taro roots) and *arh begun* (eggplant with a fish called 'arh') I ever tasted. Ten years since she last fed me, I can still taste the meals she would cook up on a shoestring budget. Rama makes the most wonderful masoor dal, shukto and pabda maccher jhol, and I am lucky that I can still sometimes get her to cook for us. In her own way, using traditional techniques and everyday ingredients, she is a genius, too.

In many ways, the chef-restaurateur is quite the image of our times, a variant of today's heroes – the inventor-entrepreneurs who take risks, innovate and change our lives forever, for better and for worse. We forgive them their self-absorption, the fact that they talk of social good when they mean their own good and their willingness to turn their backs on their loudly stated ideals when the money is big enough. All because we believe (often because they have told us) that they are touched by genius and hence connect us to the frontiers of human possibility.

The great chefs offer us the same joy, conveniently plated for immediate consumption. Not just El Bulli's foam surprises and NOMA's edible imitations of Scandinavian seascapes – not that I have been to those hallowed destinations – but also the unlikely savoury mung dal jalebi filled with fish eggs that we ate at Kolkata's wonderful Annaja.

Restaurants fit well with how economists have traditionally thought of firms. In our models, a creative spirit sets up a firm and employs all the other inputs (labour, skills, machines) to turn dream into a reality. The firm's productivity, *in this view*, mostly depends on the entrepreneur's talent and the effort he puts into making it a success, for which we pay him/her the (very) big bucks – Mr Musk claims that he needs to be paid a cool 54 billion dollars this year to ensure that he has the incentive to fight off the Chinese competition on behalf of Tesla.

The key point is that chefs cannot work alone, which makes them very different from the present-day image of the solitary artist-genius. This wasn't always the case. In the sixteenth century, Tiziano Vecellio – who we know as 'Titian' – ran a workshop where the art that we now call Titian's work was produced by a group of apprentices under his guidance. This probably meant that he needed to keep regular hours and ensure he was there when his staff was.

Very much like a chef has to. No chef alone can produce even a fraction of the food that he sells. He needs a variety of assistants who start long before the restaurant opens, making sauces, marinating meat, sculpting pastries and so on. They often each have different tasks, and the chef needs all of them to do their job perfectly before he can swing his wand and turn the dishes into the creations he is known for. For instance, the production of the elaborate, multi-layered French dessert called 'entremets', Jade tells me, can take as many as five days, with up to three people working on each entremet at the same time – the right kind of biscuit has to be made, soaked in the right syrup, combined with a mousse and crémeux (which have to be made separately) and then coated appropriately with nuts or chocolate.

But what makes running a restaurant even harder is that a client is waiting for that food, with a strong expectation that he get it within a short interval of having ordered. This means that if there has been a mistake somewhere in that chain of production, because, say, one of the new assistants did not do their job properly or the great man himself screwed up, there is no way to go back and properly paint over the mistakes. The only option is a quick fudge and then, fingers crossed, the client may just not notice.

In fact, the pressure starts many hours before the restaurant opens. The leeks did not show up, the fish was a little iffy and the ice cream melted for some reason. Time to scramble, to call in favours from other suppliers, to redesign the menu to fit what you have and still be able to pretend that things are the same.

In other words, running a successful restaurant is a huge management challenge: making sure that many people do many things at the appropriate times. And this is where the lone genius model of a chef (or an entrepreneur) starts to wear (very) thin. Good management is a lot about designing workflows that are based on realistic assumptions about what specific people can do day after day. In principle, a restaurant could choose its menu and design its entire production process to minimize the stress and excitement, by hiring enough staff so that there is always a backup and everyone has adequate time to do or (if necessary) redo any particular task.

Well-designed workflows also make it possible to delegate decisions. And delegating to the right person and trusting them to do a good job is another skill of an effective manager. This requires introspection by the chef – understanding what he does well and what is better trusted to someone else's judgement.

Good management is also about keeping the staff happy – one disgruntled restaurant worker can spell ruin for his bosses in a way that Titian's assistants never could. It is about regularly chatting with the suppliers to make sure that they can be relied upon. And about actually keeping calm and carrying on in the middle of mayhem.

The point of departure of the movies and TV shows mentioned above is that many talented chefs have no natural aptitude for this. The brilliant chef and central character in *The Bear* is a preternaturally shy young man – so frightened of life that he gives a beautiful young woman (who hits on him) a fake number – with little appetite for details or planning. As a result, disaster follows disaster, fat fires break out in the kitchen, and staff members quit, but this being a made-up story, there is a happy ending.

In real life, things do not always work out so nicely – *The New York Times* is full of notices for restaurant closures. All too often, based on the late chef and TV personality Anthony Bourdain's *Kitchen Confidential* (as well as what Jade tells us), restaurants seem to rely on the charisma of the chef and the lure of a Michelin star (or other acclaim) to get its staff to work extra hours for no extra pay and to make them forgive their boss' brattish behaviour at stressful moments. Yelling and being yelled at, making mistakes and covering them up, snorting cocaine to get through the nights when that extra bit of energy is all that stands between you and disaster, seems to be the order of all too many restaurants.

For an economist, the question is: why? The chef does not lack incentives – it is his career and fame that is on the line, and he makes money if the restaurant succeeds. So why doesn't he plan things better?

It is only recently that economists have begun to recognize that incentives are not always enough to deliver good management. Even relatively large firms often seem to be almost egregiously ill-managed. A study[21] by Nicholas Bloom from Stanford University (and four others) on Indian textile firms with 100-plus employees finds that firm managers make elementary errors. They fail to ensure that their yarn inventory is labelled, thus cannot find the yarn they need, and sometimes leave flammable material on the shop floor. This seems inconsistent with firms responding efficiently to the incentives they face; there is always excellent reason to avoid fire hazards, for example, but the managers don't always manage.

People sometimes ask me if I would like to run a restaurant. I enjoy cooking, but I am a terrible manager. Even delegating the prep work in my home kitchen to a willing volunteer stresses me out. I say no.

A well-run kitchen ought to have its stock of chutneys. They are quick to make and last several days, and can be strategically deployed to perk up an otherwise unexciting offering.

PEANUT TOMATO CHUTNEY

1½ CUPS COARSELY CHOPPED TOMATOES

1 CUP ROASTED PEANUTS

1–2 RED CHILLIES

2 TBSP OIL

1 TBSP CHOPPED GARLIC

2 TSP MUSTARD SEEDS

1 TSP CUMIN SEEDS

2 TSP URAD/CHANA DAL

A SPRIG OF CURRY LEAVES

SALT (TO TASTE)

 ▶ In a pan, heat 1 tbsp oil and throw in 1 tsp mustard seeds; when they start popping, add 1 tsp cumin seeds and 1–2 red chillies. As soon as the chillies start to brown, add 1 tbsp chopped garlic and reduce the heat. When you can smell the garlic, add 1½ cups of coarsely chopped tomatoes and salt (to taste). Cook for 5 minutes or until the tomatoes break down and become gooey. Add 1 cup of roasted peanuts and sauté for a minute. Take the mixture off the flame and once it has cooled down, put it in a blender just long enough to make it sticky.

In a pan, heat 1 tbsp oil and add 1 tsp mustard seeds to it. When they start popping, add a sprig of curry leaves and urad dal (or failing that, chana dal). Fry them for a minute and then add the chutney.

COURGETTE CHUTNEY

2 CUPS COURGETTE

½ CUP FINELY CHOPPED SHALLOTS 2 TBSP OIL

⅔ CUP FINELY CHOPPED TOMATOES

1 TBSP CHANA DAL

2 TSP CHOPPED GARLIC

2 TSP CHOPPED GINGER

1 TSP MUSTARD SEEDS

1 RED CHILLI

CURRY LEAVES

LEAVES OF CILANTRO

SALT (TO TASTE)

▶ In a pan, heat 2 tbsp of oil and throw in 1 tsp mustard seeds. When they start popping, add 1 tbsp chana dal, a few curry leaves and a red chilli. When the chilli browns slightly, add ½ cup of finely chopped shallots and let them soften at lowish heat for 3 minutes. Add 2 tsp chopped garlic and 2 tsp chopped ginger, frying them for a minute. Next, add ⅔ cup of finely chopped tomatoes along with salt. Soften the tomatoes so that you have a sauce and then add 2 cups of courgette (chopped in ½" cubes). Cover and let it cook for ten minutes, till the courgette is completely soft. Grind the whole mixture with enough stems and leaves of cilantro to fill up a cup very loosely. Check for salt.

ONION CHUTNEY

2 LARGE UNPEELED RED ONIONS

1 DRY RED CHILI

2 TBSP OIL

2 TBSP RAW PEANUTS

1½ TSP CHOPPED GARLIC

1 TSP BROWN SUGAR

1 TSP SALT

1 TSP MUSTARD SEEDS

¾ TSP LEMON JUICE (OR ⅓ TSP TAMARIND PASTE)

¾ TSP URAD DAL

¾ TSP CHANA DAL

½ TSP SUGAR

½ TSP CUMIN SEEDS

A SPRIG OF CURRY LEAVES

A PINCH OF HING

 ▶ Take two large, unpeeled red onions. Cut them into 8 wedges each and roast the wedges with a drizzle of oil. Add ¼ tsp salt and ½ tsp sugar (for caramelizing) and place the wedges in the oven at 200°C for 30 minutes (or till they are soft and sweet, based on their sizes). Take off the beards and skins of the onions.

In a 8" frying pan, heat 2 tsp of oil and fry 1 dry red chili, ½ tsp cumin seeds, 2 tbsp raw peanuts,

¾ tsp urad dal and ¾ tsp chana dal (I just used raw dried white chickpeas) till they are slightly brown, and then add 1½ tsp chopped garlic. Fry for a minute and add the onions; lower the heat and cook for 2 minutes. Take the mixture off the heat and let it cool.

Now put the mixture into a blender along with ½ cup water, 1 tsp brown sugar, ½ tsp salt and ¾ tsp lemon juice (or ideally, ⅓ tsp tamarind paste mixed with 2 tbsp water). Grind it into a nearly smooth paste. Taste for a nice balance of sweet, salty and sour, ensuring none of these dominate the flavour of the roasted onions.

In a small pan, heat 1 tbsp oil and throw in 1 tsp mustard seeds. When they start popping, add a pinch of hing and a few curry leaves. Let it sizzle for 30 seconds and pour this over the chutney.

FIG CHUTNEY

3 CUPS FIGS

½ CUP FINELY CHOPPED RED ONION

2 TBSP MUSTARD OIL

1 TBSP SUGAR

½ TBSP GRATED GINGER

½ TSP FENNEL SEEDS

½ TSP NIGELLA SEEDS

½ TSP SALT

¼ TSP METHI SEEDS

¼ TSP PIMENT D'ESPELETTE (OR DEGGI MIRCH)

▶ In a small frying pan, heat 2 tbsp mustard oil. Throw in ¼ tsp methi seeds, ½ tsp fennel seeds and ½ tsp nigella seeds. When they start sizzling, say after 45 seconds, add ½ cup finely chopped red onion. Soften the onion at medium heat for about 4 minutes. Add 3 cups of figs (chopped into eighths) and ½ tbsp grated ginger. Then, add 1 tbsp sugar (to draw the water out), ½ tsp salt and ¼ tsp piment d'espelette. Cover and cook at low heat for 12 minutes. Taste for salt and remove to a bowl.

MOOLI–ALSI KI CHUTNEY

⅓ CUP BEATEN HUNG CURD

½ GRATED DAIKON

1 TBSP FLAX SEEDS

1 TBSP CORIANDER LEAVES (FINELY CHOPPED)

1 TSP SALT (AS PER TASTE)

4 PEPPERCORNS

1" GINGER (GRATED)

1 GREEN CHILLI (THINLY SLICED)

 ▶ Roast 1 tbsp flax seeds and 4 peppercorns, and grind them into a powder. Grate ½ daikon and squeeze out the excess water in the shreds by hand.

Now, mix the grated daikon with ⅓ cup of beaten hung curd, roasted flax seeds and peppercorn powder (from the earlier step), grated ginger, a thinly sliced green chilli and 1 tbsp finely chopped coriander leaves. Set the mixture aside for 10 minutes before serving.

ROASTED GRAPE CHUTNEY

200 GM GRAPES

⅔ CUP WALNUTS

¼ CUP RED ONION

1 MEDIUM GARLIC CLOVE

3 TBSP MINT LEAVES

1 TBSP OLIVE OIL

½ TSP PAPRIKA

½ TSP SALT

½ TSP CARAWAY SEEDS

½ GREEN CHILLI

SALT (TO TASTE)

▶ Coat 200 gm grapes with 1 tbsp olive oil and salt (to taste). Roast them at 200°C for 20 minutes. In the meantime, soak ⅔ cup of walnuts in boiling water for 30 minutes.

Add the roasted grapes (along with the liquid from roasting) to a blender together with the soaked walnuts, ¼ cup roughly chopped red onion, 1 medium garlic clove, 3 tbsp mint leaves, ½ tsp caraway seeds, ½ tsp paprika, ½ tsp salt, ½ green chilli and ⅓ cup water. Blend to a smooth paste and adjust the salt if required.

Notes

1. Bursztyn, Leonardo, et al. 'Misperceived Social Norms: Women Working Outside the Home in Saudi Arabia', *American Economic Review*, Vol. 110, No. 10, October 2020, pp. 2997–3029, https://doi.org/10.1257/aer.20180975.

2. Chetty, Raj, et al. 'Income Segregation and Intergenerational Mobility across Colleges in the United States', *The Quarterly Journal of Economics*, Vol. 135, No. 3, 2 February 2020, pp. 1567–1633, https://doi.org/10.1093/qje/qjaa005.

3. 'Mental Health and COVID-19: Early Evidence of the Pandemic's Impact', World Health Organization, 2 March 2022, https://tinyurl.com/2pdz8v2c.

4. Waldfogel, Joel. 'The Deadweight Loss of Christmas', *American Economic Review*, Vol. 83, No. 5, February 1993, pp. 1328–36, https://tinyurl.com/2cxve3nx.

5. Mauss, Marcel. *The Gift: The Form and Reason for Exchange in Archaic Societies*, 1925, Translated by W. D. Halls, W.W. Norton, 1954.

6. Bryan, Gharad, et al. 'Underinvestment in a Profitable Technology: The Case of Seasonal Migration in Bangladesh', *Econometrica*, Vol. 82, No. 5, 3 October 2014, pp. 1671–1748, https://doi.org/10.3982/ecta10489.

7. Greif, Avner. 'Reputation and Coalitions in Medieval Trade: Evidence on the Maghribi Traders', *The Journal of Economic History*, Vol. 49, No. 4, December 1989, pp. 857–882, https://doi.org/10.1017/S0022050700009475.

8. Ge, Jianxiong. Unification and Division: Implications of Chinese History (统一与分裂：中国历史的启示). Beijing: The Commercial Press, 2013.

9. Zhou, Haiwen. 'Unification and Division: A Theory of Institutional Choices in Imperial China', Munich Personal RePEc Archive, Ludwig Maximilian University of Munich, 15 February 2023, tinyurl.com/mrxapd8m.

10. '"ENGLISH NEW YEAR" and OTHER POEMS by Iswar Gupta', Literary Activism, 15 January 2021, tinyurl.com/4je7j9du.

11. Atkin, David. 'Trade, Tastes, and Nutrition in India', *American Economic Review*, Vol. 103, No. 5, August 2013, pp. 1629–1663, https://doi.org/10.1257/aer.103.5.1629.

12. Imbert, Clément, and John Papp. 'Labor Market Effects of Social Programs: Evidence from India's Employment Guarantee', *American Economic Journal: Applied Economics*, Vol. 7, No. 2, 1 April 2015, pp. 233–263, https://doi.org/10.1257/app.20130401.

13. Gupta, Sarika S. 'Perils of the Paperwork: The Impact of Information and Application Assistance on Take-Up of Welfare Programs in India', 15 November 2017, https://tinyurl.com/yupt9suf.

14. Jayachandran, Seema, and Rohini Pande. 'Why Are Indian Children So Short? The Role of Birth Order and Son Preference', *American*

Economic Review, Vol. 107, No. 9, 1 September 2017, pp. 2600–2629, https://doi.org/10.1257/aer.20151282.

15. Willett, Walter, et al. 'Food in the Anthropocene: The Eat–*Lancet* Commission on Healthy Diets from Sustainable Food Systems', *The Lancet Commissions*, Vol. 393, No. 10170, 2 February 2019, pp. 447–492, https://doi.org/10.1016/S0140-6736(18)31788-4.

16. Sharma, Manika, et al. 'A Comparison of the Indian Diet with the EAT-Lancet Reference Diet', *BMC Public Health*, Vol. 20, No. 1, 29 May 2020, https://doi.org/10.1186/s12889-020-08951-8.

17. Burgess, Robin, et al. 'Weather, Climate Change and Death in India', London School of Economics, 20 April 2017, tinyurl.com/8kt5ukv3.

18. S. Iyengar, Sheena, and Mark R. Lepper. 'When Choice Is Demotivating: Can One Desire Too Much of a Good Thing?', *Journal of Personality and Social Psychology*, Vol. 79, No. 6, pp. 995–1006, https://doi.org/10.1037/0022-3514.79.6.995.

19. Veblen, Thorstein. *The Theory of the Leisure Class: An Economic Study in the Evolution of Institutions*, 1899, United States of America, Macmillan.

20. Bertrand, Marianne, and Adair Morse, 'Trickle-Down Consumption', *The Review of Economics and Statistics*, Vol. 98, No. 5, December 2016, pp. 863–79. *JSTOR*, https://tinyurl.com/nn2tjhvv, The MIT Press.

21. Bloom, Nicholas, et al. 'Does Management Matter? Evidence from India', *The Quarterly Journal of Economics*, Vol. 128, No. 1, 18 November 2013, pp. 1–51, https://doi.org/10.1093/qje/qjs044.

MORE BOOKS BY
ABHIJIT BANERJEE AND
ESTHER DUFLO

Good Economics for Hard Times

Is opening up to international trade good for everybody? Do immigrants from poorer countries take away jobs from low-income native workers? Why is inequality exploding everywhere? Does redistribution actually undermine incentives? Should we worry about the rise of artificial intelligence or celebrate it? How do we manage the trade-off between growth and climate change? Is economic growth over in the West? Should we care?

Figuring out how to deal with today's critical economic problems is the great challenge of our time. Much greater than space travel, perhaps even than curing cancer — what is at stake is the whole idea of the good life and, perhaps, of liberal democracy itself. We have the resources to solve these problems; what we lack are ideas that will help us jump the wall of disagreement and distrust that divides us. Only if we can engage seriously in this quest, and if the best minds in the world work with governments and civil society to redesign our social programs for effectiveness and political viability, will history remember our era with gratitude.

In this revolutionary book, renowned MIT economists Abhijit V. Banerjee and Esther Duflo take on this challenge, building on cutting-edge research in economics, explained with lucidity and grace. Original, provocative, and urgent, *Good Economics for Hard Times* makes a persuasive case for intelligent interventions toward a society built on compassion and respect. It is an extraordinary book, one that will help us appreciate and understand our precariously balanced world.

Cooking to Save Your Life

We all know of Abhijit Banerjee as a Nobel Prize-winning economist. Now meet Abhijit Banerjee, the gourmet chef. In this playful, erudite and sensationally delicious cookbook, Banerjee takes us through the recipes he has delighted his friends, colleagues and students with – from charred avocado to Andhra pork ribs, deconstructed salade niçoise to a trifle made in under 20 minutes. Along the way, he riffs on Karl Marx, Bengali vegetarian cooking and why soup is so consoling. Superbly illustrated by Cheyenne Olivier, this is a book to both read and to cook outstanding meals from.

Poverty and Income Distribution in India

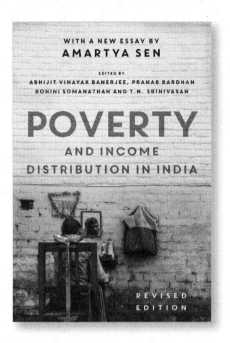

Poverty and Income Distribution in India, first published in 1974, brought together the global who's who of poverty research of that time. But over the years, out of print, this important book had essentially vanished from library collections around the world.

With four new essays by the present editors and one by the economics Nobel laureate Amartya Sen, which reflect on the shifts in perspective that have taken place in the decades gone by, this updated volume is an essential reference. Offering insights into conceptual and practical issues in the measurement of poverty, it is indispensable for students and practitioners alike.

This book also redresses a bias in the intellectual history of modern social sciences, which is skewed towards the West. The ideas coming out of India were a major influence on the spread of survey methods across the world after 1950: indeed, this may be the single most important contribution and influence of India on the social sciences. A group of Indian economists and statisticians based at institutions like the Indian Statistical Institute and the Delhi School of Economics led the world in thinking about issues of poverty, all the way from what causes and constitutes poverty to how to measure it and collect reliable data about it. This book tries to reclaim that proud moment in India's intellectual history.

What the Economy Needs Now

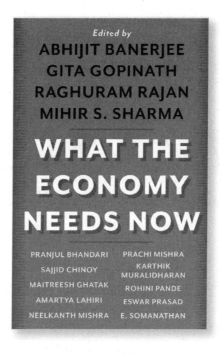

India's economy is under threat with rising unemployment, banks in crisis, falling GDP and farmers' unrest making headlines daily. In this brilliant and urgent book, the country's most important economists – including Abhijit Banerjee, Gita Gopinath and Raghuram Rajan – bring together their proposals on how to get the country back on track. Collectively the book provides solutions to the key problems that India is currently facing – labour reforms, healthcare, education and the environment – while also focusing on the vital economic growth of the nation. Rigorously yet accessibly argued, *What the Economy Needs Now* is a timely and deeply important book.

Poor Economics for Kids

Nilou lives in a village. She and her friends are just like you – they don't like going to school and they love playing on tablets – but many of her experiences aren't like yours. The pharmacy nearby doesn't have all the medicines they need; during a flood, some of her friends lose their homes, and when her favourite cousin can't find work in the village, he has to go to the city to make a living. In this fun, smart, and beautifully illustrated book, Esther Duflo and Cheyenne Olivier weave a series of delightful stories that will open your eyes to the world around you.